W9-AVK-994

Practical Cataloguing
AACR, RDA and MARC 21

WITHDRAWN

Practical Cataloguing
AACR, RDA and MARC 21

Anne Welsh and Sue Batley

Neal-Schuman
An imprint of the American Library Association
Chicago   2012

Schaumburg Township District Library
130 South Roselle Road
Schaumburg, IL 60193

9/12
Amaz
.75 00

TS OFFICE
R
025.32
WELSH, A

3 1257 02407 5961

Published by Neal-Schuman, an imprint of the American Library Association
50 E. Huron Street
Chicago, IL 60611
www.neal-schuman.com

© 2012 Anne Welsh and Sue Batley

All rights reserved. Reproduction of this book, in whole or in part, without written permission of the publisher, is prohibited.

First published in the United Kingdom by Facet Publishing, 2012.
This simultaneous U.S. edition published by Neal-Schuman, an imprint of the American Library Association, 2012.

Printed and made in the United Kingdom.

The paper used in this publication meets the minimum requirements of American National Standard for Information Sciences—Permanence of Paper for Printed Library Materials, ANSI Z39.48-1992.

Library of Congress Cataloging-in-Publication Data

Welsh, Anne, 1972-
    Practical cataloguing : AACR, RDA and MARC 21 / Anne Welsh and Sue Batley.
        p. cm.
    Published simultaneously in the United Kingdom by Facet Publishing.
    Includes bibliographical references and index.
    ISBN 978-1-55570-743-9 (alk. paper)
    1. Descriptive cataloging—Handbooks, manuals, etc. 2. Resource description & access—Handbooks, manuals, etc. 3. Anglo-American cataloguing rules—Handbooks, manuals, etc. 4. MARC formats—Handbooks, manuals, etc. I. Batley, Sue. II. Title.

Z694.W425 2012
025.3'2—dc23
                                                                    2012000552

Dedication

For my parents
Anne Welsh

For my mum
Sue Batley

Contents

Acknowledgements

This book was written at a time of flux in international cataloguing standards, and would not have been possible without the help, encouragement and support of many people inside and outside the library profession. Although the responsibility for the text is entirely our own, it was built on a lot of excellent cataloguing advice.

In particular, thanks are due to the trio of professional cataloguers working at the coalface who have generously shared their opinions on RDA informally: Celine Carty, Thomas Meehan and Helen Williams. Thank you for keeping cataloguing grounded, vital and fun. For more formally expressed opinions, thanks to the speakers at CILIP's RDA Executive Briefings 2010 and 2011 and to Jason Russell for making these events happen.

Thanks also to UCL cataloguing students 2009–2011 and to Janet Barratt and her team at Manchester John Rylands. There is nothing like having to discuss a new cataloguing standard with intelligent, engaged librarians to clarify one's own opinions and thoughts. Kate Whaite deserves a special mention. At the other end of the profession, the 'old guard': you know who you are and what is owed.

Finally, but with most direct impact on there actually being a book, thanks to Marc Mathison and Helen Carley. You both know why.

Anne Welsh
January 2012

Preface

This book has been three years in the making. It was commissioned to bridge the gap between John Bowman's *Essential Cataloguing* (last published before MARC revised its series fields from 440 and 490 to 490 alone) and Shawne Miksa's North American textbook on the new international cataloguing standard *Resource Description and Access*, to be published in the UK in 2013 (Miksa, n.d.).

It aims to meet the needs of two markets:

- those trained in cataloguing under *Anglo-American Cataloguing Rules* 2nd Edition (AACR2) in need of a refresher, especially in the light of the new standard
- those being trained in the current environment, when AACR2 is being phased out and the new standard is being phased in.

I use the verb 'trained' advisedly here. In the UK, there are few library schools that *teach* cataloguing in any detail. At the last comprehensive survey in 2005, University College London (UCL) was found to be the last in the UK with a *compulsory* module on cataloguing and classification, consisting of ten weeks of practical experience using AACR2 and several classification schema, which can be followed by an optional module 'Advanced Cataloguing & Classification'.

This does not mean that cataloguing is completely absent from the UK's library schools. Many teach information architecture, incorporating a more *theoretical* knowledge. Students leave knowing what cataloguing is and how it aids information retrieval. They can recognize what a catalogue record looks like and have an understanding of the principles of knowledge organization.

Practice in actual cataloguing – picking up a book (or other item), analysing it, describing it and providing access to it – is a little harder to come by.

Recent issues of CILIP's *Catalogue & Index* highlight the range of experience on library and information science (LIS) courses in 2011 (Carlton, 2011; Grim, 2011; Maule, 2011). Issue 162 includes an account by a student who spent three years at library school without, he says, cataloguing anything, but who actively sought volunteer experience outside university to learn how to catalogue (Carlton, 2011). In issue 163, a UCL student mentions a more theoretical course she took in the USA, and describes her determined and deliberate approach to gaining cataloguing experience – through taking the MA LIS at UCL and obtaining volunteer and paid work during her year in London (Howard, 2011).

Outside the published literature, I know cataloguers who speak of library school cataloguing experiences including 'optional lunchtime sessions, in which, in one lunch hour, AACR2 was passed round and discussed', and one of my professional friends taught herself, 'reading the rules and asking colleagues for advice'.

For a generation – since the demise of compulsory cataloguing at library school nationwide – aspiring UK cataloguers have used Bowman's *Essential Cataloguing* (2007). Work through it, with AACR2 open on your desk and the MARC manual on your desktop, and you will succeed in learning the basics. I don't speak from personal experience here – I *learned* cataloguing in my pre-library school year at St Deiniol's (now Gladstone's) Library and at library school in Aberystwyth, where it was still a core module. But I *trained* people using Bowman when I was a cataloguer myself, and it remains the back-stop for my teaching at UCL. Ignore the now outdated section on series, and Bowman still gives good cat.

Practical Cataloguing does not aim to replace Bowman entirely. Reference is made to *Essential Cataloguing* at various points. Nor does it aim to *teach* cataloguing in the way that North American textbooks do. Sue Batley and I *teach* cataloguing within our different MA programmes. Teaching involves a more theoretical academic approach. At UCL, roughly ten hours are spent on cataloguing theory to contextualize around 20 hours of hands-on experience.

Books on cataloguing theory abound. My personal favourite is Lois Mai Chan's *Cataloging and Classification* (2007), although I also recommend Arlene Taylor's *Introduction to Cataloging and Classification* (2006). My students also read appropriate sections of Cutter's *Rules for a Dictionary Catalog* (1891), and in one session we look at that hybrid catalogue *par excellence*, the *British Museum Catalogue*, considering the evolution of cataloguing from Mr Panizzi's Rules.

In more recent years, IFLA (International Federation of Library Associations and Institutions) has given us *Functional Requirements for Bibliographic Records* (1998), the fairy godmother of Resource Description and Access (RDA), and in class we use Arlene Taylor's writings on the subject, as well as William Denton's terrific chapter 'FRBR and the history of cataloging' (2007).

Other favourite authors and commentators among UCL students include Karen Coyle and Michael Gorman, while hot topics of student discussion at the moment are linked data, crowdsourcing and the open data movement. Each year at least one student is inspired by Gordon Dunsire's work.

Practical Cataloguing does not aim to stand *in lieu* of all of this good theory. Nor is it a substitute for reading the many cataloguer blogs out there – most of them collated in Planet Cataloging at http://planetcataloging.org.

In short, this is not a course syllabus, nor a workbook. Sue and I each have our own versions of these, as we are sure other lecturers in cataloguing do. Instead, *Practical Cataloguing* sets out to highlight the most common issues encountered by cataloguers and suggests resolutions for these issues. It aims to be used in conjunction with AACR2, RDA and MARC 21, but also alongside cataloguing policy and training manuals from individual institutions and cataloguing consortia, and best practice guidelines from the national and leading libraries.

If you have been plunged into the world of cataloguing and want to (re)orientate yourself; if you have taken over responsibility for cataloguing policy in your institution; or if you have started studying cataloguing at university and you would like a pragmatic approach, *Practical Cataloguing* is the book for you.

If the acronyms in this preface and on the title page of this book are just so much meaningless jargon to you; if you don't like using the catalogue in your own library; or if you just don't see why a Google-style algorithm can't 'fix' your bibliographic records, *Practical Cataloguing* will set you on the right path and point you to sources for further information.

Practical Cataloguing will suggest a sensible time frame and route to decisions for library managers who are wondering whether, how or when they need to move to the new cataloguing standard they have been hearing about (RDA).

One final *caveat*: at the time of publishing (March 2012), only three libraries have adopted RDA. The Library of Congress has listened to arguments from their testers that they need to continue to practise their RDA skills, and so some RDA records will also be encountered in the Library of Congress catalogue, but these are very much in the minority. The Library of Congress has stated that it will not adopt the new standard until January 2013 at the earliest, and then only once certain changes have been made to it. This means that while the other sections in the book represent around 20 years of cataloguing experience in the real world, the sections on RDA are based on observations of cataloguing over the last year. We, like you, await further documentation from the national libraries; further statements from the Joint Steering Committee responsible for RDA; and the creation of a corpus of catalogue data in RDA by library practitioners in the real world.

Anne Welsh
Lecturer in Library & Information Studies
University College London

1

Catalogues and cataloguing standards

Catalogue. 1. (Noun) A list of books, maps or other items, arranged in some definite order. It records, describes and indexes (usually completely) the resources of a collection, a library or a group of libraries. To be distinguished from (i) a list, which may or may not be in any particular order and may be incomplete, and (ii) a bibliography, which may or may not be confined to any one collection of books or to a particular group of libraries. Each entry bears details of class number or call number to enable the item to be found, as well as sufficient details... to identify and describe the book. 2. (Verb) To compile a list of documents according to a set of rules so as to enable the consulter to know what items are available and... where they may be found.

(Prytherch, 1995)

This working definition from a standard glossary of library terms encompasses in broad brush the focus of this book, which is to outline general cataloguing principles and highlight the major rules through which those principles are commonly applied within library collections.

In 2011/12 library cataloguing is in a state of flux as a new international cataloguing standard, *Resource Description and Access* (RDA), is developed and introduced (Joint Steering Committee for the Development of RDA, 2011). Widespread consultation and discussion underpins this committee-developed standard, and cataloguers and library managers await with interest each draft, toolkit and, eventually, implementation guidance.

At times like this, it is more important than ever that cataloguers should understand the general principles for providing information to their users, in order, ultimately, to decide on local cataloguing policy for their libraries.

In this introductory chapter, we will consider the roots of general cataloguing principles and briefly survey the history of the development of the codes that are in use today.

Ranganathan

For many librarians, Ranganathan's Five Laws form the basic principles of librarianship:

- Books are for use.
- Every book its reader.
- Every reader his book.
- Save the time of the reader.
- A library is a growing organism.

(Ranganathan, 1957)

It is easy to relate these laws to cataloguing, which renders items findable ('Books are for use' and 'Every reader his book') quickly and efficiently ('Save the time of the reader') and performs an inventory function for the library's stock ('Every book its reader' and 'A library is a growing organism').

Indeed, in his later publication, *Classified Catalogue Code*, Ranganathan went on to state that the catalogue:

Should be so designed as to:

- Disclose to every reader his or her document;
- Secure for every document its reader;
- Save the time of the reader; and for this purpose
- Save the time of the staff.

(Ranganathan, 1989)

Ranganathan is also a good place to start when we think about general cataloguing principles, since his laws place the user at the centre of the library, and it is important to remember this when we catalogue – a well prepared catalogue record may be a beautiful thing to the trained eye, but the true measure of its worth must be in its value to those searching it in finding information.

Cutter

In fact the major aims and objectives of the cataloguer have changed little since the 19th century, when Cutter outlined the objects and means of library cataloguing:

Objects
1. To enable a person to find a book of which either
    A. the author
    B. the title
    C. the subject is known
2. To show what the library has
    D. by a given author
    E. on a given subject
    F. in a given kind of literature
3. To assist in the choice of a book
    G. as to its edition (bibliographically)
    H. as to its character (literary or topical)

Means
1. Author-entry with the necessary references (for A and D).
2. Title-entry or title-reference (for B).
3. Subject-entry, cross-references, and classed subject-table (for C and E).
4. Form-entry (for F).
5. Notes (for G and H).

Reasons for Choice
Other things being equal, choose the entry
1. That will probably be the first looked under by the class of people who use the library;
2. That is consistent with other entries, so that one principle can cover all;
3. That will mass entries least in places where it is difficult to so arrange them that they can be readily found, as under names of nations and cities.

(Cutter, 1891)

In recent years, Cutter's objects have been reflected in the user tasks set out by the *Functional Requirements for Bibliographic Records* (FRBR), an international initiative which in turn has greatly influenced RDA (IFLA, 1998). In FRBR, the attributes and relationships within a catalogue are mapped to user tasks that form the core aims of the record, and which are:

- to *find* entities that correspond to the user's stated search criteria
- to *identify* an entity
- to *select* an entity that is appropriate to the user's needs
- to acquire or *obtain* access to the entity described.

In 2009, IFLA published an updated *International Statement of Cataloguing Principles* (IFLA Cataloguing Section and IFLA Meetings of Experts on an International Cataloguing Code, 2009), which built on the work of FRBR and asserted 'This first principle is to serve the convenience of catalogue users'.

So we can see that the objectives of cataloguing have remained constant for over a century.

Lubetzky

The final 'Great Man of Cataloguing' whom we will consider here is Seymour Lubetzky, who in the mid-20th century developed principles that took a 'back-to-basics' approach. His attitude is arguably extremely relevant today, when we are faced with a complex and ever-changing environment, with new formats and materials to document and, as for Lubetzky, a complicated matrix of cataloguing codes and standards from which we can choose.

As Lois Mai Chan has put it, in Lubetzky's *Studies of Descriptive Cataloging* (1946), *Cataloging Rules and Principles* (1953), *Code of Cataloging Rules* (1960) and *Principles of Cataloging* (1969), he insisted on 'a rationalised approach to cataloging standards based on objectives and principles [that] laid the foundation for subsequent cataloging code development. He is credited for transforming cataloging codes "rich in rules" to those "rich in principle"' (Chan, 2007).

As our own standards change radically over the next few years, it is arguably the case that all those responsible for cataloguing policy will need to adopt a similar streamlining approach.

The Paris Principles, ISBD, AACR, RDA

Drawing on the work of Lubetzky, the Paris Principles or Paris Statement came out of an international conference held in 1961. The discussions at this conference led to the first edition of the *Anglo-American Cataloguing Rules* (AACR), which was published in 1967. In 1969 a further set of meetings was held in Copenhagen, which led to the development of International Standard Bibliographic Description (ISBD).

ISBD covers a range of standards, the first being *ISBD (M): International Standard Bibliographic Description (for single volume and multi volume monographic publications)*, originally published in 1971. There have been many others, covering such resources as cartographic materials (ISBD (CM)), electronic resources (ISBD (ER)) and serials (ISBD (S)). ISBD is one of the codes that underpins the MARC format.

Since its publication in 1978, AACR2 has had three further incarnations: AACR2R (1988), which consolidated the three supplements to AACR2 issued in the 1980s; AACR2R (1998), which dealt with numerous amendments to the code; and AACR2R (2002), which as well as covering minor changes throughout, also incorporated substantial coverage of electronic resources.

The Joint Steering Committee for the Revision of AACR, which wrote and administered the AACR, decided in 2005 that the changes that it was making to AACR2 had sufficiently wide implications that the next edition would be better to be published under the new title *Resource Description and Access* (RDA).

Constituency consultation fed into the new code, published in online format in June 2010. Although they bowed to pressure from the cataloguing community and issued a print version, members of the Joint Steering Committee and the lead publisher, the American Library Association (ALA), have stressed that, unlike previous codes, RDA has been conceived from the start as an online text, and online access is required to receive the full benefits of the code.

So this is where we find ourselves in 2012. After over 30 years of cataloguing using the same code, we are looking at radical changes to our practice. The Library of Congress has been running extensive tests, which will lead not only to decisions about implementation, but also guidance on how implementation might be achieved. Meanwhile, the Machine-Readable Bibliographic Information (MARBI) Committee, responsible for MARC, has started to introduce changes to make the implementation of RDA possible in a consistent way for libraries using MARC 21 format.

This book examines the implications of the new code, compares it to the existing standards and, more importantly, highlights the roots of AACR2 and RDA in general cataloguing principles. It also provides some guidance on the major format for bibliographic description, MARC 21. Finally, it provides examples of materials commonly encountered in modern library cataloguing, and gives suggestions for how these might be handled (see Chapter 10).

2

The FRBRization of the catalogue

Functional Requirements for Bibliographic Records (FRBR) was first published in 1998 (IFLA, 1998) and, as the commentator William Denton has pointed out, 'is an end point of almost 175 years of thinking about what catalogs are for and how they should work – *an* end point, not *the* end point' (Denton, 2007).

While carrying on the tradition of the supremacy of the user's convenience established by Cutter, FRBR is concerned with the intellectual concept of the *work* – the concept of the book (or video or piece of music) – and its relationship to the copies that are held by individual libraries.

The word 'work' has been used throughout the history of cataloguing with more or less specificity. Panizzi, the most famous of the keepers of the British Museum Library, was concerned with the relationships between different versions of books, asserting that 'a reader may know the *work* he requires; but he cannot be expected to know all the peculiarities of different *editions*, and this information he has a right to expect from the catalogues' (Lubetzky and Svenonius, 2001).

Indeed, such questions have been central to much enumerative and analytical bibliography over the years, with academics and rare books librarians documenting not only editions but also impressions and states of early printed books (Gaskell, 1995) and provenance information at the individual copy level of rare materials (Pearson, 1998).

In making the convenience of the user its first principle, FRBR goes on to consider how the user's needs might best be served. As Barbara Tillett has put it, 'Especially important are the efforts libraries make to help users find resources by uniquely identifying the resources through bibliographic description and by collocating or gathering together resources that share some common characteristic. These are usually resources in a library's own collections, but sometimes bibliographic descriptions or pointers are provided to resources beyond its collections' (Tillett, 2007).

Relationships at the heart of the catalogue

FRBR suggests that the library catalogue should do more than enable the location of a particular item. In essence, in creating a 'FRBRized' catalogue record, we are describing not only the thing we have in our hands, but its relationship to other things in the bibliographic universe – not only to its creator(s) and previous editions, but, theoretically, to any other thing that may be of use to an end user.

For those of us trained under the old model of cataloguing, in which we described something and provided access to it through a limited number of fields, this can sound scary. After all, most of us are working in libraries with collection policies, so viewed from one angle we could argue, theoretically, that all the things collected by the library are related to one another, one way or another. Where then should our process of documentation (cataloguing) end?

A pragmatic way to think about how FRBR fits into cataloguing theory is to say that it goes back to basics in much the same way Cutter did. Like Cutter, it focuses first and foremost on the information that we can *predict* what the end user wants to know – the ways in which the catalogue user would like to search for information. This thought is calming, as we can observe straight away that the march of technology has increased the ways in which users can search, and so 'all' that is required is for us to put this technology to good use and provide catalogue records that exploit the advantages of new ways of searching.

The advance of technology has also increased the array of 'things' users seek. These are no longer just books and journals. They are not even floppy disks (for those of us old enough to remember them). They are things that have become much less embodied – computer programs, for example. The word processing software on which this book's manuscript was typed is available pre-installed on a Mac or a PC, on a CD-ROM, on a DVD and as a download. Gone are the days when the software and the thing embodying it are inseparable.

And the 'things' users seek are not just new-fangled things like computer programs. With the advent of the e-journal and the e-book, all librarians (not solely those of us concerned with rare books) are having to think about the book as object; the book as container; the book as text; and, significantly here, the book as concept. In the last two to three years there has been a rise in the number of queries to the cataloguing listservs about how to handle e-journals and e-books.

A recent listserv debate concerned the loaning of e-book readers preloaded with a selection of texts: should the reader be catalogued with the texts rendered in the contents note area and with added title entries? Or was that duplicating the records already extant on the library catalogue for the e-books themselves? What was the library user borrowing exactly, and should it have two records (one for the reader and one for its contents) or one composite record (for both the reader and its contents) or, as several cataloguers pointed out, should the reader not be catalogued at all, but be logged and checked out using an equipment list?

When online content, such as digitized images of collection items, was first created, a common pragmatic solution was simply to create a link to the digital version from the catalogue record for the paper (or vellum) item. This assumed that the catalogue user was interested in content not form – that, for example, a digital image of an early New Testament was either exactly the same as the printed version it reproduced, or that for the purposes of most catalogue users it could be treated as the same.

Scholarship in Digital Humanities has taught us the limits of this apparent 'sameness'. Teaching students Historical Bibliography, it quickly becomes clear how much they need to rely on the original printed item to detect the style of printing (woodcut versus lithograph, for example) and that in a digital image it can sometimes be difficult to detect when something has been written or drawn in later (where we can simply feel the indentation on a printed page to know if the printing press has weighed down on it to create the mark).

That's not to belittle the use of digitization. As a technology it has allowed greater access to content (especially over the internet), and in some cases has enabled us to read items that could not be read by the human eye – as, for example, in the case of the Vindolanda tablets (Terras, 2006). On the contrary, a digitized version of something is not merely a digital copy of it. It truly is a different version and cannot and should not be seen as interchangeable with the printed item.

In brief, FRBR acknowledges that each object a user seeks consists of content and form and that each of these may be of interest to users. Beyond that, it recognizes that the different versions of an object can, and often do, have complex relationships.

Works, expressions, manifestations and items

At base, FRBR asserts that a **work** 'is realized through [an] **expression** [which] is embodied in [a] **manifestation**, [which] is exemplified by [an] **item**' (IFLA Study Group on the Functional Requirements for Bibliographic Records, 2009).

This can be difficult to grasp without a concrete example. Tom Delsey suggested a few, which are available in MARC's 'Displays for multiple versions from MARC 21 and FRBR' available at www.loc.gov/marc/marc-functional-analysis/multiple-versions.html (Library of Congress Network Development and MARC Standards Office, 2003). Section 4.3 at www.loc.gov/marc/marc-functional-analysis/multiple-versions.html#english-patient provides examples for two texts and one sound recording of Michael Ondaatje's novel *The English Patient*, along with works related to it – the motion picture and the screenplay.

Later in the same document, we are presented with the MARC records and a suggested hierarchical display, which, in turn, Thomas Meehan has offered in a more visual format at www.aurochs.org/frbr_example/frbr_example.html (Meehan, [2010]).

In each of these different displays, we see that the **work** entitled *The English Patient* is realized through 1. **expression** as a text in English and 2. **expression** as a sound recording in English. The first expression (text) is embodied in two **manifestations**: 1. published by Chivers in 1997 and 2. published by Vintage in 1993. The second expression (sound recording) is embodied in a **manifestation** produced by Macmillan Audio in 1997.

Clearly, the film is a **work** in its own right, although it is related to Ondaatje's book. It is realized through **expression** as a motion picture and embodied in **manifestation**s 1. Miramax Home Entertainment videodisc, 2. Miramax Home Entertainment laserdiscs and 3. Miramax Films on 18 reels.

Finally, the screenplay forms a **work** that is related both to Ondaatje's book and Minghella's film. It is realized through **expression** as text in English and embodied in a **manifestation** published by Hyperion Miramax Books.

In our modern world it is not difficult to think of hundreds of books that, like *The English Patient*, have inspired films; TV series that have given birth to books and short stories; and computer games that have been translated into films, books and even toys. FRBR aims to facilitate the modelling of such complex relationships.

Because of its ability to conceptualize relations between different entities, FRBR was identified as a useful model for the 21st century's new cataloguing code, and you can read more about its role as the foundation of *Resource Description and Access* (RDA) in Chapter 5.

One final online resource that you may like to explore at this early stage is Variations FRBR, which describes itself as 'a testbed for the FRBR conceptual model' – www.dlib.indiana.edu/projects/vfrbr/. We'll return to it again in Chapter 5, but if you want to play around with catalogue records that have this type of relationship expressed, and gain some insight into how a FRBRized catalogue might look, Variations FRBR is a good place to start.

Relationships to people

Of course, publications are not solely related to each other. Most proudly declare their relationships to people too – authors, editors, illustrators, directors, producers and performers to name only a few. And these people may be related to each other: Cassandra Austen was Jane Austen's sister, Admiral Francis Austen was their brother, and their letters to and from each other could be described as being by the Austen family.

In recent years, both within and outside the library community, a great deal of time and effort has been put into working out relationship models between people. The growth in social networking sites, such as MySpace and Facebook, has provided computer scientists and sociologists with new information about how human beings relate to each other – how we represent ourselves online and create our digital identities.

Meanwhile, the growth of the crime of identity theft has made it important to be able to identify people accurately online, and the banking and security industries have invested heavily in research in these areas. Personal identification has become big business (Higgs, 2011).

As a result there is much that cataloguing theorists and practitioners can learn from the wider world. Further, as well as being the product of technological change, the ID industry has evolved several technological innovations, which we can see slowly making their way through to library management systems.

At its core, the information sector remains interested in two activities: identifying the person or people involved in the creation of a publication, and disambiguating that person or those people from others with the same name. Indeed, at conferences and other professional gatherings, cataloguers often point out that one advantage of a library catalogue over the big search engines is its ability to differentiate and disambiguate.

So we see that the John Smith involved in the establishment of Virginia (born 1580, died 1631, 111 books by or about him on the Library of Congress catalogue) is listed separately from the John Smith who wrote the biography of English comedian Benny Hill (born 17 December 1936, only one book by him on the Library of Congress catalogue). That might not sound so remarkable, but the same library database (http://authorities.loc.gov) differentiates between the John Smith who wrote *The Benny Hill Story* and the John Smith born earlier in the same year (5 May 1936), who wrote *Primary Education and Libraries* (Liverpool Polytechnic, 1979), which is not held by the Library of Congress, although the name record is ready for it, should it ever be accessioned there.

Chapter 4 discusses this library concept of name authority in more detail, with examples of how it is used in relation to AACR2, and then it is picked up again in the chapters dealing specifically with MARC 21 and RDA. What is important to recognize here is that within the world of library cataloguing a lot of manual work has been carried out to create international databases of names that relate to publications.

Of course, the concept of the 'publication' is one that, arguably, has changed since the birth of the internet. The word 'publishing' used to be used to describe a time-consuming and skilled process whereby a book or article was written, edited, printed and offered for sale. Since the mid-20th century such items carried international standard book numbers (ISBNs) or international standard serial numbers (ISSNs) and formed the main content of libraries and library catalogues. Now we talk about 'publishing' a pdf (portable data file) by posting it to the internet. Similarly, we upload videos, podcasts and photographs – all of them 'published' in the sense of being made publicly available and all of them possibly of use to library users.

Some libraries have retained a view that they will include in their holdings and/or their catalogue only traditionally published materials. Some have decided that such materials should be available through the library, but not directly through the catalogue – a common solution is to implement a meta-search engine (sometimes called a discovery engine) that searches catalogue records and other web-based resources selected by the information professionals employed by the library. Most libraries that lack the resources to purchase, implement and manage a meta-search facility, add records for pdf and other web-based resources – either printing off and creating local copies of the resource and/or linking to them on the internet, but in either case, creating some sort of catalogue record for them.

As a result there has been an exponential growth in the number of people whose names might qualify for inclusion in library catalogues. The manual system for creating name records cannot cope with the entire internet and its millions of authors.

What can libraries do? Should we develop an approach similar to our professional neighbours in the archive community? Archivists have always had to cope with creating name headings in an environment in which literally anyone might author a document and therefore require a name heading. The archival standard Encoded Archival Description (EAD) is expressed in Extensible Markup Language (XML) and includes a range of tags for names, including <name>, <persname>, <corpname> (for organizations) and <famname> (Library of Congress Network Development and MARC Standards Office and Society of American Archivists, 2011).

Or should we wait for the International Standard Name Identifier (ISNI), currently offered as a public draft by the International Standards Organization – draft ISO 27729 – to be fully published and implemented? The scope of this initiative is 'the identification of Public Identities of parties: that is, the identities used publicly by parties involved throughout the media content industries in the creation, production, management, and content distribution chains' (www.isni.org).

'What is a "public identity"?' you might ask. The ISNI turns straight away to the world of books for examples: 'A Public Identity is the name by which a Party is publicly known. For example, Lewis Caroll is the Public Identity of a natural person called Charles Lutwige Dodgson. A Party can be a natural person (a human being), a legal entity (such as a company) or a fictional character such as Peter Pan' (www.isni.org).

One of the most important things to note about the ISNI initiative is that it aims to provide each Public Identity with a number code, similar to an ISBN for a book or an ISSN for a journal. The website offers examples to illustrate this principle, although with the caveat that 'The Public Identities on the page are just samples and MAY NOT BE USED' (ISNI International Agency, [2011]). The first example concerns one of the many John Smiths, in this case allocated the sample ISNI 000 1000 0000 1774, and show as First Name: John; Last Name: Smith; Class: Literary; and Role: Author. Other classes and roles exemplified include Musical Work | Composer; Literary | Publisher; Audio Visual | Actor; and Visual Arts | Photographer.

The use of a number as the identifier aims to surmount challenges of language and display, and it is important to grasp that the modern development in name control and display is less about generating a heading and more about collocating all the different names by which an entity (in FRBR terms) or Public Identity (in ISNI terms) might be known. Modern library management systems are sophisticated enough (in theory, at least) to ingest identities in numeric form and display them in the language and character set of the cataloguing agency or user.

Another important international initiative is the Virtual International Authority File (VIAF) Project (http://viaf.org), hosted by the Online Computer Library Center (OCLC) with contributions from agencies including the National Library of Australia, Bibliotheque nationale de France, Deutsche Nationalbibliothek, Library of Congress and Name Authority Cooperative Program (NACO), Library and Archives Canada and several other national libraries, alongside specialist libraries including the Getty Research Institute and Vatican Library. VIAF aims 'to lower the cost and increase the utility of library authority files by matching and linking widely used authority files and making that information available on the Web' (http://viaf.org).

Like ISNI, the VIAF Project is concerned not solely with preferred name headings, but with collocating variant forms of names. Moving towards facilitating linked data about names within the semantic web, VIAF is open about '(1) allowing national and regional variations in authorized form to coexist; and (2) supporting needs for variations in preferred language, script and spelling' (OCLC Research, March 2011).

The FRBR community has been working on the display of names and the relationships between people, organizations and publications for a number of years. In September 2008, the IFLA Cataloguing Section approved the findings of a review led by Barbara Tillett into the feasibility of an International Standard Authority Data Number (ISADN). Key among the recommendations was that 'IFLA should continue to monitor the progress of efforts of the ISO 27729 ISNI Working Group and the VIAF Project and any potential numbering that may result from those efforts. IFLA member institutions should also actively seek to influence the ISNI with a view to identifying common purposes with other communities' (Tillett, 2008).

This review is just one output from an ongoing concern with authority data shown by IFLA since the publication of FRBR in 1998. In 2005, IFLA released its draft *Functional Requirements for Authority Records: a conceptual model* (FRAR). This seminal work defined relationships that have formed the foundations for subsequent modeling on the run up to the creation of RDA.

So FRAR delineates that a work, expression, manifestation or item as described in FRBR 'is associated with [a] person, family [and / or] corporate body'. These entities are 'known by [a] name [and] assigned [an] identity'. This name and identity form the 'basis for [the] access point[s]'. You can read more about access points from Chapter 3 onwards – they are a core concept within cataloguing, and discussed in detail in AACR2, MARC and RDA. As FRAR pointed out, access points have to be 'governed by rules [which are] applied by [an] agency'. Cataloguers spend a lot of time deciding on the access points for the items on which they are working. Conceptually, 'access' is half the job. (The other half is, of course, description.)

The latest publication from IFLA on name headings and the relationships between people and works was issued in 2009. The successor to FRAR, *Functional Requirements for Authority Data: a conceptual model* (FRAD) (Patton, 2009) was released in draft form in 2007, and both the draft and the final version fed into the conception of entities in RDA. It should be noted that although FRAR and FRAD identify non-personal entities (concept, event, object and place), which are also carried through to RDA, the work that has been done so far focuses very much on the entities of person, family and corporate body.

Just like FRBR, FRAD identifies user tasks: to find, identify, contextualize and justify. The first two tasks are, hopefully, obvious. The last is administrative – the creator of the authority record should be able to 'justify' (in other words document) their reason for choosing the name and form of heading they have selected.

Arguably the most important of the four tasks to grasp at this point is that of contextualization. The modern authority file should seek to contextualize the publications of the person, corporate body or family, but also should clarify the relationship between the family, corporate body or family and the name(s) by which they are known (Patton, 2009).

Like ISNI, FRAD, therefore, seeks to collocate the names by which someone, an organization or a family is known. These currently have to be collocated under an authorized heading, but remember Tillett's 2008 recommendation that IFLA should continue to monitor the development of ISNI. Perhaps within our professional lifetimes as cataloguers we will see the adoption of ISNI within our library catalogues. More excitingly, perhaps we will see our library authority data forming a basis for ISNI's files of Public Identities.

Practice note

These first two chapters have been theoretical in nature. The concepts highlighted not only underpin the decisions made by those who create our cataloguing codes (AACR2 and RDA) and data exchange formats (MARC 21) but, if we take time to understand them, can also form the foundations for a strong understanding of the aims and objectives of cataloguing. The rest of this book is concerned with the practical implementation of these general principles.

3

Bibliographic elements

A bibliographic description, whether created using AACR2, RDA or any other set of cataloguing rules, is composed of a series of individual bibliographic elements. As well as telling the catalogue user the title of a work and who created it, for example, some of those elements specify and describe the physical manifestation of the item.

This means that the publication format of the item being described influences the content of parts of the catalogue record. One of the primary drivers for the change in cataloguing standards is the proliferation of new physical storage media and e-formats, which have led to challenges to accommodate them in bibliographic description.

Format first

Many of the issues encountered in AACR2 stem from its being based upon pre-computer age principles (mainly to suit the card catalogue). Critics charge it with placing too much emphasis on publication format – and, indeed, following a general section that outlines general principles applicable to any and all formats (Part I-1), the rest of Part I is taken up with rules relating to specific formats:

1   General Rules for Description 1-1
2   Books, Pamphlets, and Printed Sheets 2-1
3   Cartographic Materials 3-1
4   Manuscripts (Including Manuscript Collections) 4-1
5   Music 5-1
6   Sound Recordings 6-1

(Joint Steering Committee for the Revision of AACR, 2005)

This structure means that before cataloguing an item we have to decide what format it takes, and then apply rules from the relevant sections of AACR2. For example, a paperback edition of the latest Dan Brown thriller is catalogued following I-1 (General Rules) and I-2 (Books, Pamphlets, and Printed Sheets), while the video of his first blockbuster, *The Da Vinci Code*, is catalogued following I-1 and I-7 (Motion Pictures and Videorecordings). Cataloguers quickly get into the habit of following this structure, which can be summed up as *follow I-1 (General Rules) except when you are instructed to do something else in a later, format-specific section.*

This has been taken even further with regard to some formats. For example, rare books cataloguers have further extended AACR2, first with *Descriptive Cataloguing for Rare Books* and more recently with *Descriptive Cataloguing for Rare Materials (Books)*, while map cataloguers have developed *Cartographic Materials: a manual of interpretation for AACR2*. These developments are sometimes seen as a tacit criticism of AACR2 for not being specific enough in its treatment of certain formats, but AACR2 is regularly defended as a general code with guidance for some formats, and some specialist cataloguers feel that it is not the role of the general code to deal with the more specialist aspects of their practice.

Other criticisms levelled at AACR2's structure include:

- *Repetitiveness* – if a rule is not general enough to be included in I-1, but applies to more than one format, the only option is to repeat the rule in each section to which it applies.
- *Fragmentation* – it has been possible for some cataloguers to specialize in one or two formats and be unaware of the rules for other formats. For example, the intricacies of 'I-12 Continuing Resources' often remain a

mystery to those without a current or previous role looking after serial publications.

- *Privileging of 'the Book'* – most courses on basic cataloguing teach students how to catalogue books, partly because that is the format most commonly encountered by general cataloguers, and partly because it is easy to provide print-based examples from which students can work. As well as providing easily portable homework, authorized photocopies of title pages and their versos (backs) become an *aide memoire* for students, who can annotate their example packs based on work with the real books and further example items in class.

By far the biggest criticism of AACR2's structure is that any list of publication formats is, by its nature, finite. It is argued that in the 21st century our cataloguing code should provide general rules that are infinitely extensible and can be applied not only to existing formats, but also to any new format that may arise in future.

RDA is not structured in format-specific sections, but is based on the principle of providing general rules with exceptions and options for various circumstances, one of which, where relevant, is publication format.

Based on the documents circulated for consultation, there has been a mixed response, with cataloguers:

- favouring the change, as leading to a more coherent structure, giving more examples from different formats, and providing confidence to move from a format with which they have experience (e.g. books) to ones in which they do not (e.g. electronic resources)
- disliking the change, as taking a structure they found straightforward and compartmentalized and 'cluttering it up' with concepts and examples that do not apply to the format(s) they themselves catalogue; this viewpoint has been loudly stated, and given that the majority of cataloguers (and certainly non-MA LIS qualified cataloguers) work solely with books, this is hardly surprising
- being unsure whether their initial dislike of the new code and its structure stems from being so used to the old structure of AACR2; some cataloguers have, of course, been using AACR2 for nearly 40 years.

A fourth position that was voiced during the free-trial phase of the RDA Toolkit (the online product through which RDA is accessed) was that cataloguers were not sure whether they liked or disliked the new code more because of the online nature of its access and presentation.

Chapter 8 discusses the current state of play in implementing RDA. In June 2011, the Library of Congress announced that it will implement RDA in 2013, following some amendments to the standard (Library of Congress, National Agricultural Library and National Library of Medicine, 2011). Given the importance of publication format traditionally and with regard to interoperability with other databases, it should come as no surprise that three fields dealing with format issues, Content Type, Carrier Type and Media Type, have already been added to MARC. It should be noted that in May 2011, the Library of Congress announced an investigation into the role of MARC and the possibilities of moving to another format, which if used with RDA could increase facilities for linked data (Library of Congress Network Development and MARC Standards Office Bibliographic Framework Transition Initiative, 2011). So, in the next five years, there will be a transition in the way that we catalogue.

It is enough to note here that the first practical decision we make to help us catalogue items using AACR2 is deciding what type of publication we have in front of us.

Identifying the bibliographic elements

With cataloguing practice in transition from AACR2 to RDA, a beginning cataloguer might be well advised to look beyond the individual codes to identify the major bibliographic elements.

International Standard Bibliographic Description (ISBD) is a lynch-pin of universal bibliographic control – the ability to share records at a truly international level. The preliminary edition of *Full ISBD Examples* (IFLA, 2009) highlights why it is so useful. Records are shown in 16 different languages, including those using non-Roman characters, for example Arabic, Korean and Japanese. Even if we cannot read the language or script, we can identify the different areas of the catalogue record, because they are shown in the same order, with the same punctuation.

International Standard Bibliographic Description (General) (ISBD(G)) specifies eight elements for bibliographic description, which identify a particular work and which differentiate it from other works:

1   Title and statement of responsibility area
2   Edition area
3   Material (or type of publication) specific area
4   Publication, distribution, etc. area
5   Physical description area
6   Series area
7   Note area
8   Standard number (or alternative) and terms of availability area.

(IFLA Committee on Cataloguing ISBD
Review Committee Working Group, 1992)

AACR2 and MARC 21 have been designed to be compatible with ISBD, and it is possible to build on an understanding of the principles of these elements with the specifics of each set of rules and the MARC format. One of the chief criticisms raised against RDA internationally is that it does not always take account of the specifics of ISBD. It is difficult to imagine that, after decades of international co-operation on ISBD, the Joint Steering Committee will not be pressurized by the Library of Congress and the wider cataloguing community into adopting a closer proximity to ISBD. In the interim, the workflows in the RDA Toolkit allow for the arrangement of RDA rules by ISBD area. Beginning cataloguers are, therefore, strongly recommended to form an understanding of general principles based on ISBD, as a building block towards understanding AACR2, MARC 21 and RDA.

The ISBD areas also map neatly to Cutter's objects and means discussed in Chapter 1, with the addition by ISBD of areas for series and standard numbers (e.g. ISBNs and ISSNs).

Title and statement of responsibility

The title is one of the most important pieces of information for identifying a publication. Although some publications, such as images, may not have a title inherent within them, a general rule of thumb is that most things have a title.

Titles provide an access point to the item, and this aspect will be discussed in the next chapter. For now, we want to concentrate on the title as a vital part of the *descriptive area* of the catalogue record.

Title proper

We are clearly instructed in both AACR2 and RDA to *transcribe* information from the title page as accurately as possible. In this, we are performing the function of creating a *surrogate* of the publication, ideally providing the catalogue user with enough information to conjure a picture in their mind's eye of how the title page has been set out.

AACR2 1.1B1 instructs us to 'Transcribe the title proper exactly as to wording, order, and spelling, but not necessarily as to punctuation and capitalisation... capitalise according to appendix A'.

Flicking to the back of AACR2, we see that the standard rule is **AACR2 A.4A1**: 'In general, capitalise the first word of a title... Capitalise other words as instructed in rules for the language involved.'

In English, this means that we capitalize only the first word of the title and then any proper nouns within it. We ignore the design choices of the publisher, which often capitalizes every noun in a title on a title page.

If you look at the title pages in Chapter 10 and their records, you can see this in action. For example:

Essential cataloguing
Centuries of skin
The wounded deer
Noble deeds of the world's heroines

Other examples include:

| Title page: | THE PLEASURES OF PARIS |
| Entered as: | The pleasures of Paris |

| Title page: | IN THE FOOTSTEPS OF ADAM |
| Entered as: | In the footsteps of Adam |

| Title page: | *Treasury of* CHRISTMAS COOKING, CRAFTS, *and* GIFTS |

| Entered as: | Treasury of Christmas cooking, crafts and gifts |

| Title page: | ABC FOR BOOK COLLECTORS |
| Entered as: | ABC for book collectors |

AACR2 1.1B1 goes on to give some exceptions to exact transcription: 'If the title proper as given in the chief source of information includes the punctuation marks... or [ ], replace them by – and (), respectively.'

This is because we use '...' as a marker for text we have omitted and we enclose any insertions in square brackets '[ ]'.

| Title page: | Why does my rabbit... ? |
| Entered as: | Why does my rabbit – ? |

Other title information

Referred to colloquially as a *subtitle*, other title information elaborates on the title proper. In Chapter 10, the fourth example provides a classic example of other title information. Looking at the title page, we can see that the title 'everything we don't say' is added to further down the page by the word 'poetry', which is useful to the catalogue user as it explains that this is a collection of poems, and not a self-help book about failures in communication.

It is important to distinguish other title information from a part title, which splits a publication up into several volumes: 'Volume 3'; 'A–M'; 'the early years' are all likely to indicate a part of a work.

It is also important to distinguish other title information from publisher's puff. In recent years, it has not been uncommon to see hyperbolic statements normally reserved for the dustjacket or cover creeping onto the title page. In the film *Bridget Jones' diary*, Bridget may have had to introduce 'Kafka's motorbike, the best-written book of all time', but as cataloguers we would hope that the tagline stayed on the posters and cover and did not make it onto the title page. Even if it did, we would happily ignore it.

Epigrams and epigraphs on the title page are, similarly, not other title information, and should be ignored.

Once we are certain we are dealing with other title information, we precede it with space colon space and, as instructed by **AACR2 1.1E5**, 'Transcribe other title information following the whole or part of the title proper.'

So, our example from Chapter 10 becomes:

Everything we don't say : poetry

These are other examples from Chapter 10:

The wounded deer : fourteen poems after Frida Kahlo
Unconcerned but not indifferent : the life of Man Ray : poems

Note that in the final example, there are two pieces of other title information, so we precede each with 'space colon space'.

Further examples of other title information:

Title page:	IMAGINED LONDON
	A Tour of the World's Greatest Fictional City
Entered as:	Imagined London : a tour of the world's greatest fictional city

Title page:	A YEAR IN A Scots Kitchen
	CELEBRATING SUMMER'S END TO WORSHIPPING ITS BEGINNING
Entered as:	A year in a Scots kitchen : celebrating summer's end to worshipping its beginning

Title page:	Strange Fruit
	Billie Holiday, Café Society, and an Early Cry for Civil Rights
Entered as:	Strange fruit : Billie Holiday, cafe society and an early cry for civil rights

Title page:	THE FIFTEENTH-CENTURY BOOK
	THE SCRIBES ◉ THE PRINTERS ◉ THE DECORATORS
Entered as:	The fifteenth-century book : the scribes, the printers, the decorators

Statement of responsibility

The statement of responsibility is a useful piece of jargon that indicates the part of the title page that tells us the people and/or organizations involved in creating the item.

(N.B. The statement of responsibility is concerned solely with *description*. We provide *access* by name in the author and added author access points of the record, dealt with in the next chapter.)

AACR2 1.1F1 instructs us to 'Transcribe statements of responsibility appearing prominently in the item in the form in which they appear there'.

Common ways to recognize a statement of responsibility include:

- the word 'by'
- the words 'edited by'
- the words 'illustrated by'
- the word 'photographs:'
- *no indicative words or punctuation, but the typography distinguishes it.*

We precede the first statement of responsibility with an oblique, as in these examples from Chapter 10:

Essential cataloguing / J. H. Bowman

Centuries of skin / Joanna Ezekiel

Everything we don't say : poetry / Jasmine Ann Cooray

Noble deeds of the world's heroines / by Henry Charles Moore

We precede subsequent statement of responsibility with a semi-colon:

Title page:	PADDINGTON HERE AND NOW *by* MICHAEL BOND *illustrated by* R.W. ALLEY
Entered as:	Paddington here and now / by Michael Bond ; illustrated by R.W. Alley
Title page:	*Weeds and Wild Flowers* Poems by Alice Oswald Etchings by Jessica Greenman

Entered as:	Weeds and wild flowers / poems by Alice Oswald ; etchings by Jessica Greenman

The order of precedence of statements of responsibility is determined by the order in which they appear on the title page. Sometimes, beginning cataloguers have a tendency to prioritize the author of any text, but **AACR2 1.1F6** is quite clear: 'If there is more than one statement of responsibility, transcribe them in the order indicated by their sequence on, or the layout of, the chief source of information. If the sequence and layout are ambiguous or insufficient to determine the order, transcribe the statements in the order that makes the most sense.'

Another fairly common complication by which the beginning cataloguer can be confused is where the publisher has deviated from the standard order of title followed by statement(s) of responsibility for design reasons. **AACR2 1.1F3** deals with this:

'If a statement of responsibility precedes the title proper in the chief source of information, transpose it to its required position unless it is an integral part of the title proper.'

So in these cases, we change the order:

Title page:	*Michael Bond*
	Paddington At Work
	With drawings by Peggy Fortnum
Entered as:	Paddington at work / Michael Bond ; with drawings by Peggy Fortnum

Title page:	Paddington
	Michael Bond
	A Classic Collection
	With drawings by Peggy Fortnum
	Coloured by Caroline Nuttall-Smith
Entered as:	Paddington : a classic collection / Michael Bond ; with drawings by Peggy Fortnum ; coloured by Caroline Nuttall-Smith

These are examples of statements of responsibility that are integral to the title proper:

| Title screen: | *Mary Shelley's Frankenstein* |
| Entered as: | Mary Shelley's Frankenstein |

Title page:	Robin Ince's
	Bad Book Club
	One Man's Quest to Uncover the Books that Taste Forgot
Entered as:	Robin Ince's Bad Book Club : one man's quest to uncover
	the books that taste forgot

AACR2 1.1F2 instructs us not to insert a statement of responsibility if it is not present in the chief source of information: 'If no statement of responsibility appears prominently in the item, neither construct one nor extract one from the content of the item. Give relevant information in a note.'

Practice note

Be aware that some libraries deviate from this, and do insert a cataloguer-constructed statement of responsibility in square brackets when one is not given in the chief source of information.

The rule of three

This fundamental of cataloguing under AACR will change with the introduction of RDA, but remain as an option, so it is important to take note of it as both the current 'norm' and an option that we may predict will continue in some libraries under RDA.

AACR2 1.1F5 instructs us:

> If a single statement of responsibility names more than three persons or corporate bodies performing the same function, or with the same degree of responsibility, omit all but the first of each group of such persons or bodies. Indicate the omission by the mark of omission (...) and add *et al.* (or its equivalent in a nonroman script) in square brackets.

So in this example, only the first author, Damian Chalmers, is credited in the catalogue record:

Title page:	EUROPEAN UNION LAW
	TEXT AND MATERIALS
	DAMIAN CHALMERS
	CHRISTOS HADJIEMMANUIL
	GIORGIO MONTI
	ADAM TOMKINS
Entered as:	European Union Law : text and materials / Damian Chalmers ... [et al.]

Under RDA, the title field would include all four authors (unless the rule of three option were retained in the catalogue on which we were working):

European Union Law : text and materials / Damian Chalmers, Christos Hadjiemmanuil, Giorgio Monti, Adam Tomkins

AACR2 1.1F7 deals with titles of nobility and qualifications:

Include titles and abbreviations of titles of nobility, address, honour and distinction, initials of societies, qualifications, date(s) of founding, mottoes, etc., in statements of responsibility if:

(a)   such data are necessary grammatically

(b)   the omission would leave only a person's given name or surname

(c)   the title is necessary to identify a person

(d)   the title is a title of nobility, or is a British term of honour.

Librarians of a certain age in the UK and North America will remember with fondness (or otherwise) the novels of Miss Read, which presented a chocolate-box picture of English village life to the world. Without the 'Miss' in the statement of responsibility, we would be left with the odd-looking entry:

Battles at Thrush Green / Read

So, of course, AACR2 is logical to instruct us to enter it as:

Battles at Thrush Green / Miss Read

And of course, the less cosy Marquis de Sade would retain his title of nobility:

The crimes of love / Marquis de Sade

Alternative titles

AACR2 1.1B1 defines the alternative title as 'part of the title proper... Precede and follow the word *or*... introducing an alternative title by a comma. Capitalize the first word of the alternative title.'

It includes a few examples, including

Marcel Marceau, ou, L'art du mime

Under the hill, or, The story of Venus and Tannhäuser

Practice note

This rule is often ignored or forgotten by cataloguers, as we can see in this example from a real catalogue:

The annotated Hobbit: the Hobbit, or There and back again ... 2003
The hobbit: or there and back again ... 1982, c1981
The hobbit: or there and back again ... 1989
The Hobbit: or there and back again ... 1991, c1937

Parallel titles

We can recognize parallel titles quite easily: the title appears on the chief source of information in more than one language.

AACR2 1.1D instructs us:

1.1D1 Transcribe parallel titles in the order indicated by their sequence on, or by the layout of, the chief source of information.

1.1D3 Transcribe an original title in a language different from that of the title proper appearing in the chief source of information as a parallel title if the item contains all or some of the text in the original language...

So a text of Gunther Grass's classic novel *The tin drum* that contained the text in English and German would be entered as:

The tin drum = Die Blechtrommel

In this case, we would normally enter a language note:

Text in English and German.

Note the use of the '=' mark as punctuation. Beginning cataloguers often find this one of the easiest to remember in AACR2, the equals sign being a common way to represent parallelism outside the world of cataloguing rules.

Practice note

It is not uncommon to find catalogue records where the parallel title form of entry has been used for items that appear in only one language but have a translation of the title alone into another language. In effect, the cataloguer has used the parallel title entry form as a 'workaround' for an oddity in publishing, where another cataloguer might ignore the title in a different language, arguing that other than the title, the work does not include 'all or some of the text in the original language'.

Edition area

The edition statement is one of the most straightforward rules in AACR2:

1.2B1. Transcribe the edition statement as found on the item. Use abbreviations as instructed in appendix B and numerals as instructed in appendix C
  e.g. *2nd ed.*

Abbreviations

From Appendix B:

edition	ed.
editions	eds.
revised	rev.
corrected	corr.

Watch out for these (not covered):

abridged

expanded

updated

Statements of responsibility

1.2C1. Transcribe a statement of responsibility relating to one or more editions, but not to all editions, of a given work following the edition statement if there is one...

1.2C2. In case of doubt about whether a statement of responsibility applies to all editions, or only to some, or if there is no edition statement, give such a statement in the title and statement of responsibility area.

Source of information

Unlike the title, which we are instructed to take from the title page, for monographs, we can take edition information from the title page, other preliminaries or the colophon (**AACR2 2.0B2**). In most modern books, we find edition information on the title page or title page verso, as shown in the following examples:

Title page: CUB SCOUTS

Who they are and what they do

by DAVID HARWOOD

with illustrations by

	JOHN BERRY
Facing title page:	Revised edition
	© LADYBIRD BOOKS LTD MCMLXX
Title entered as:	Cub scouts : who they are and what they do / by David Harwood ; with illustrations by John Berry
Edition entered as:	Rev. ed.

Title page:	Prejudices and Antipathies
	A Tract on the LC Subject Heads Concerning People
	by
	SANFORD BERMAN
	THE 1993 EDITION,
	WITH A FOREWORD BY ERIC MOON
Title page verso:	Copyright © 1971, 1993
Title entered as:	Prejudices and antipathies : a tract on the LC subject heads concerning people / by Sanford Berman
Edition entered as:	1993 ed. / with a foreword by Eric Moon
Note entered as:	Previous ed.: 1971.

Title page:	KEEP THE ASPIDISTRA FLYING
	BY
	GEORGE ORWELL
	SECKER & WARBURG
Title page verso:	*First published in England 1936 by Victor Gollancz Limited*
	Published in this uniform edition1954 by MARTIN SECKER & WARBURG
Title entered as:	Keep the aspidistra flying / by George Orwell
Edition entered as:	Uniform ed.
Note entered:	Originally published: Gollancz, 1936.

Title page:	Thesaurus construction and use: a practical manual
	Fourth edition
	Jean Aitchison
	Alan Gilchrist
	David Bawden
Title page verso:	© Aslib 1972, 1987, 1997, 2000

Title entered as: Thesaurus construction and use : a practical manual / Jean
Aitcheson, Alan Gilchrist, David Bawden
Edition entered as: 4th ed.
Note entered as: Previous ed.: 1997.

Title page: *Notes on a Scandal*
ZOE HELLER
Penguin Books
Title page verso: First published by Viking 2003
Published in Penguin Books 2004
Title entered as: Notes on a scandal / Zoe Heller
Edition entered as: [New ed.]
Note entered as: Originally published: Viking, 2003.

RDA does not favour the use of abbreviations. **RDA B.4** instructs us: 'For
transcribed elements, use only those abbreviations found in the sources of
information for the element. If supplying all or part of a transcribed element,
generally do not abbreviate words.'

RDA 2.5.1.4 instructs us to 'Transcribe an edition statement as it appears
on the source of information. Apply the general guidelines on transcription
given under **1.7 RDA**', which in turn directs us to **RDA B.4**.

So while AACR2 records comply with the format of the examples above,
RDA records would spell out the edition statements in full:

Title page: Revised edition
AACR2:   Rev. ed.
RDA: Revised edition

Title page: Fourth edition
AACR2:   4th ed.
RDA: Fourth edition

Publication area

At its most basic, the publication area can be divided into three components:
place; name of publisher or distributor, etc.; and date.

Place

In **AACR2 1.4C** we are instructed: 'Transcribe a place of publication, etc., in the form and grammatical case in which it appears.' For most items, this is straightforward:

London
Chicago
Sydney

Sometimes, though, it is necessary to distinguish one place from another with the same placename, as described by **AACR2 1.4C3**: 'If the name of a country, state, province, etc., appears in the course of information, transcribe it after the name of the place if it is considered necessary to distinguish the place from others of the same name.' We can also 'supply the name of the country, state, province, etc. if it does not appear in the source of information'. We should 'use abbreviations' set out in Appendix B.14:

Paris, France
London [Ont.]

An increasingly common feature in modern, global publishing is for more than one place of publication to appear. **AACR2 1.4C5** limits the number of places we need to include in our catalogue record:

> If two or more places in which a publisher, distributor, etc., has offices are named in the item, give the first named place. Give any subsequently named place that is given prominence by the layout or typography of the source of information. If the first named place and any place given prominence are not in the home country of the cataloguing agency, give also the first of any subsequently named places that is in the home country. Omit all other places.

Title page:	McFarland & Company, Inc., Publishers
	Jefferson, North Carolina, and London
In the USA,	
entered as:	Jefferson, N.C.

In the UK,
entered as: Jefferson, N.C. ; London
Elsewhere,
entered as: Jefferson, N.C.

Title page: PENGUIN BOOKS
Title page verso: Published by the Penguin Group. Penguin Books Ltd, 80
                     Strand, London WC28 0RL, London, Penguin Group (USA)...
                     New York, New York... Penguin Group (Canada)... Toronto,
                     Ontario... Penguin Ireland... Dublin... Penguin Group
                     (Australia)... Camberwell, Victoria... Penguin Group (NZ)...
                     Auckland... Penguin Books (South Africa)... Johannesburg
In the UK,
entered as: London
In the USA,
entered as: London ; New York, N.Y.
In Canada,
entered as: London ; Toronto
In Ireland,
entered as: London ; Dublin
In Australia,
entered as: London ; Camberwell, Vic.
In New Zealand,
entered as: London ; Auckland
In South Africa,
entered as: London ; Johannesburg
Elsewhere,
entered as: London

It is important to note that **RDA 2.8.2.4** favours the transcription of *all* places of publication. This is a simpler rule, easier for beginning cataloguers to understand, and which is in keeping with the global nature of information and, importantly of sharing data: no longer do South African cataloguers have to amend UK-created data to reflect their local imprint.

Practice note

Some cataloguers and managers have declared themselves vehemently opposed to this change, especially those processing large quantities of data with multiple places of publication. This is a workflow issue that will be ironed out following RDA's implementation across diverse libraries, but today it is too early to judge how many libraries will choose, for workflow reasons, to stick to the AACR2 practice.

Sometimes place of publication or distribution is given. This is especially common in videos and DVDs, but also occurs in books. **AACR2 1.4C6** instructs us:

> If the place of publication, distribution, etc., is uncertain, supply the probable place... followed by a question mark.
>
> [Munich?]
>
> ... If no place or probable place can be given, give s.l. (sine loco)...
>
> [S.l.]

RDA does not like abbreviations, particularly Latinate ones, and we are instructed in **RDA 2.8.2.6** to give instead 'Place of publication not identified'.

Name of publisher, distributor, etc.

One of the AACR2 rules with which beginning cataloguers often struggle relates to name of publisher. **AACR2 1.4D2** tells us: 'Give the name of a publisher, distributor, etc., in the shortest form in which it can be understood and identified internationally.'

So, using the examples above from the place section:

Title page:	McFarland & Company, Inc., Publishers
Entered as:	McFarland

Title page:	PENGUIN BOOKS

Entered as: Penguin

RDA 2.8.4.3 prefers transcription of the name in full, so in these examples, the name would be entered exactly as it appears on the item itself.

Practice note

Many libraries use a controlled list of publishers, so that entries in this field are consistent. They feel it helps their users to locate all the items produced by a particular publisher and that it makes bibliographies printed from the database (and the display on screen) look neater. These libraries are likely to be hostile to the move towards full transcription in this field, and, again, we will have to wait and see what happens after 2013 when the Library of Congress adopts RDA. On the other hand, libraries with rare books that use DCRM(B) are already recording full information in the publisher area, and so may prefer the RDA approach.

If no name is given, **AACR2 1.4D6** tells us to 'give *s.n.* (sine nomine)':

[s.n.]

Under **RDA 2.8.4.7**, '[s.n.]' becomes 'Publisher not identified'.

Date of publication

AACR2 1.4F1 instructs us to 'give the date (i.e. year) of publication... of the edition, revision, etc., named in the edition area... Give dates in Western-style Arabic numerals'.

   AACR2 1.4F2 continues, 'Give the date as found in the item even if it is known to be incorrect. If a date is known to be incorrect, add the correct date', for example:

1697 [i.e. 1967]

We have to be careful with dates. Often there is a long list of different dates on the back of the title page. In this area, we are not interested in reprinting of impressions – we need to ascertain the date of the particular edition we have in our hands.

Even though a publication may have been reprinted in 2011, it may have been released by the same publisher, in the same form, apart from the cover art, for 50 years. In such a case, the date we need to enter is 1961.

It is common for the same work to be published at different times by more than one publisher. We are only interested in this area in the publication we hold in our hands. Details of a previous edition or the original publisher and date can be included as a note.

It takes time, practice and experience for beginning cataloguers to develop confidence in their ability to interpret date information, as these examples show:

Title:	Dated & datable English manuscript borders c.1395-1499 / Kathleen L. Scott. Bibliographical Society ; British Library
Title page verso:	© The Bibliographical Society 2002
	First published in 2002 by the Bibliographical Society and The British Library...
Interpretation:	This is the first publication of this book, and this is set out in a clear publication statement, backed up by a clear copyright date.
Date entered as:	2002

Title:	Collected poems / Walter de la Mare. Faber and Faber.
Title page verso:	First published in 1979 by Faber and Faber Limited...
	Reprinted 1986...
	©1979 by the Literary Trustees of Walter de la Mare
Interpretation:	This is a straight reprint, with a really clear statement backed up by the copyright statement. A quick examination of the book itself reveals no new material that has been added since 1979.
Date entered as:	1979

Title:	Dewey death / Charity Blackstock. Ballantine.
Title page verso:	Copyright ©1958 by Charity Blackstock...
	First Ballantine Books Edition: December 1963

	Second printing: October 1985
Interpretation:	Here we have a reprint (in 1985) of a book published in 1963. The copyright date is somewhat earlier, and if we had the time, we might look online for the original publication date to enter into the notes field. This is a matter of local workflow and policy.
Date entered as:	1963

Title:	Oscar's books / Thomas Wright. Vintage.
Title page verso:	Published by Vintage 2009...
	Copyright © Thomas Wright 2008...
	First published in Great Britain in 2008 by Chatto & Windus...
Interpretation:	This book has been published by the Random House Group, by its Vintage imprint. A change in imprint, even when they are both owned by the same parent company, is significant enough for us to take the second date.
Date entered as:	2009
Note entered as:	Originally published: Chatto & Windus, 2008.

Title:	Who the hell is Pansy O'Hara? : the fascinating stories behind 50 of the world's best-loved books / Jenny Bond & Chris Sheedy
Title page verso:	Published by the Penguin Group...
	Copyright © Jenny Bond and Chris Sheedy, 2008
Interpretation:	It is fairly common now for books to have a copyright date and no clear statement of publication date.
Date entered as:	c2008

Title:	The system of objects / Jean Baudrillard ; translated by James Benedict. Verso.
Title page verso:	First published by Verso 1996
	This edition published by Verso 2005
	Translation © James Benedict 1996, 2005
	First published as *Le système des objects*
	© Editions Gallimard 1968

Interpretation:	This book has both a clear publication statement, backed by a corresponding copyright statement. It is a 2005 edition of a 1996 translation of a book first published in French in 1968.
Date entered as:	2005
Note entered as:	Previous ed.: 1996.

RDA places much more emphasis on copyright date. In AACR2, we usually only record a copyright date when there is no publication statement. Under **RDA 2.11.1.3**, we are expected to record the copyright date wherever it is given, so some records will have a copyright date and a publication date. Also, RDA expects us to use the copyright symbol © instead of the abbreviation 'c'.

The final date format to bear in mind is useful for cases where no date is given explicitly on the item, but we know, or we have an idea of, the date. Where we *know* the date from elsewhere (our own experience or a website, for example), we can enclose it in square brackets.

In our example *Noble deeds of the world's heroines* in Chapter 10, no date appears on the item itself. However, the book is covered by the British Library catalogue, which, as a UK copyright library, is an authoritative and reliable source of this kind of information:

Date entered as:	[1903]
Note:	Date from British Library catalogue.

If no authoritative source can be found, but we know a date, it can be entered in the same format, with an explanatory note. For example, in 2008, the UK newspaper the *Guardian* gave away a CD called *Great poets of the 20th century*. The recording, the printing on the CD and its sleeve do not mention 2008 at all. We know when we acquired the CD ourselves, and although the Guardian Books website does not mention the CD, it mentions the series, confirming our record that it was acquired in 2008:

Date entered as:	[2008]
Note:	Date from acquisition record.

Sometimes we may be less sure, in which case we might make an educated guess. It is important to do this only where it will be really helpful to the catalogue user, where we feel confident we will not mislead them. Indications could include the fabric of the book or its contents. Under **AACR2 1.4F7**, we can use short dashes to represent digits in a date and, if we are really unsure, we can indicate this with a question mark:

Date entered as:	[194-?]
Note:	Printed on highly acidic 1940s paper.

Date entered as:	[20--]
Note:	Covers the history of the 21st century, indicating a publication date after 1999.

RDA 2.8.6 directs us to **RDA 1.9.2** for the options available to us. These include a date range (**RDA 1.9.2.4**):

[between 1970 and 1979?]

Punctuating the publication, distribution, etc. area

You can refer to Chapter 10 for examples of full catalogue records, but having spent so much time discussing the variations in individual components of this area, it might be worthwhile to bring a few specific examples together.

Clear publication statement, one place of publication, one publisher:

Publication area:	London : Faber, 1979

Clear publication statement, one place of publication, one publisher, clear statement of original publisher:

Publication area:	London : Vintage, 2009
Note:	Originally published: Chatto & Windus, 2008.

No publication statement, but clear copyright statement, one publisher with two places of publication:

Publication area: New York, NY ; London : Penguin, c2008

Clear publication statement, two publishers both publishing in the same place:

Publication area: London : Bibliographical Society ; British Library, 2002

Physical description area

At this point in AACR2 we need to consult the individual chapters for the formats we are describing because this is the area that varies most between formats – obviously the physical properties of a book are different from those of a DVD.

In RDA we will have to use Chapter 3, describing carriers. The same content may be issued in a range of different formats, and RDA's separation of content and carrier information means that multiple descriptions of publication format can be attached to a single description of content, which is much more economical than creating entirely new descriptions for each item.

This area contains four elements in AACR2, all of which are present in a much more detailed form in RDA's 21 elements:

- extent of item
- dimensions
- series area
- note area.

Extent of item

RDA 3.4.1.1 defines 'extent' as 'The number and type of units and/or subunits making up a resource. A unit is a physical or logical constituent of a resource '... a subunit is a physical or logical subdivision of a unit.' It is in this element that AACR2 includes the specific material designation (SMD) described earlier. RDA has a separate area for carrier type, which essentially serves the same function. SMD or carrier type is the 'unit'. In AACR2 books and manuscripts do not require an SMD; in RDA a book needs to be assigned both a media type and a carrier type: unmediated, volume.

The extent of the item in subunits, in the instance of a book, is the number of pages or leaves. For collections of printed sheets or manuscripts we include the number of items in the collection with an explanatory term: 20 sheets, 20 items. For modern printed books we simply check the pagination and record the value of the last numbered page. Any preliminary pages with roman as opposed to arabic numerals should also be noted: xxv, 250 p.

If the pages of the work are not numbered then the approach differs. Using AACR2 we should provide a value or approximate value enclosed in square brackets: [70] p., [ca. 200] p. Using RDA we can include a simple statement to indicate lack of pagination: 70 unnumbered pages, approximately 200 pages. As in other examples, when using AACR2 a prescribed abbreviation must be used; when using RDA you don't have to abbreviate terms like pages.

For all other formats this element contains the number of items plus the SMD or carrier type: 1 sound disc, 1 globe, 2 videodiscs, 1 online resource. At this point the rules diverge again. In AACR2, for media such as sound recordings and videorecordings (music and film) we would provide information about running time in this element, either exact or approximate: 1 sound disc (72 min.), 2 videodiscs (ca. 150 min.). So the extent of the item refers to its duration. The definition of a subunit in RDA precludes this use of the term and it is not appropriate to include the number of tracks, etc. here:

AACR2:	xxiv, 367 p.
RDA:	xxiv, 367 pages
AACR2:	1 videodisc (ca. 127 min.)
RDA:	1 videodisc

The same applies to data that is embedded in the next part of this area in AACR2: other physical details. This is where you would note anything special or unusual about the item or anything that enriches it. For books that would include whether there are illustrations and whether they are in colour.

You should not record any information that is redundant. Most people expect a DVD of a feature film to have sound and to be in colour so it is not necessary to state that it is. It would be worth recording that the content of a DVD was in black and white: 1 videodisc (60 min): b&w. If the material an item is made from is unusual, special or integral to it, then you should record it here: 1 vase: glass; 1 sound disc (40 min.): mono. In RDA some of this additional information is now separated out and placed in the 'describing content' fields, other elements have been assigned specific fields within Chapter 3: for example, Configuration of playback channels: 3.16.8 mono; Encoding format: 3.19.3 DVD video. On balance this is a positive step: the more detailed structure and guidance is useful in assisting the cataloguer in describing the physical characteristics of newer media types.

Dimensions

The two sets of rules converge again in this element. Dimensions of course refer to size and you will usually need a ruler or tape measure at this point. For books it is the height of the book rounded up to the nearest centimetre. **AACR2 2.5D1** tells us that if the item is less than 10cm in height, we should give the height in millimetres. **AACR2 2.5D2** instructs us: 'If the width of the volume is either less than half the height or greater than the height, give height x width.'

Unlike vinyl recordings where it was important to distinguish between 7, 10 and 12 inch discs, most CDs and also DVDs are a standard size so it is redundant to record their dimensions – allowable in RDA because this element is optional. Obviously if anything is not a standard size then that has to be noted:

AACR2:   xxiv, 367 p. ; 23 cm.
RDA: xxiv, 367 pages, 23 cm.

The physical description area has had a major overhaul in the new rules. The more basic structure of AACR2 in this area couldn't successfully accommodate newer publication formats. Important information about the physical characteristics of items ended up in the notes area.

RDA has tackled this problem by separating format from the description of content which allows for greater depth of detail. A problem is that fields containing information about physical characteristics of items are still scattered throughout the record.

Series area

AACR2 offers three definitions of the term 'series' in its glossary, of which we are chiefly interested in the first: 'A group of separate items related to one another by the fact that each item bears, in addition to its own title proper, a collective title applying to the group as a whole. The individual items may or may not be numbered.'

It can sometimes be tricky to differentiate between a series and a multi-part item. AACR2's definition can be helpful: 'Multipart item. A monograph complete, or intended to be completed, in a finite number of separate parts.' Classic examples of multi-part items include encylopedias and dictionaries. They are finite, their size limited by the length of the alphabet by which they are arranged, and there is a strong link between each of their parts.

At the other end of the spectrum, classic series like Penguin Classics and Oxford's World Classics represent strong branding exercises on the part of the publisher – there is no 'final' part envisaged, and the series style basically incorporates any piece of literature deemed to be part of the canon.

Sometimes, beginning cataloguers can find it hard to imagine why users might be particularly interested in the series. Practical examples include lay subjects where the series style can assist in selection, such as Collins Family Pet Guides – if you found the rabbit book useful for caring for one sort of small animal, you are probably going to like the guinea pig book whenever you acquire a companion for your bunny. Even more extreme examples can be found in romantic fiction – the branding of Mills & Boon's many different series is so strong that readers will subscribe to a series rather than the work of an individual author. Silhouette is similarly orientated around a model of series.

Within the series area, there are several elements that we record:

- *Title proper of series* – this is often the only element you will need to include in this area.
- *Series subtitle* – transcribe as you would in the title proper area (some libraries have a local policy not to include a subtitle).
- *Statements of responsibility relating to series* – in some cases, although individual works in a series have separate authors or editors, the series as a whole is the responsibility of a named person or persons or body; if so, their details should be recorded following the rules for statements of responsibility.

- *Numbering within series* – if the item has a numeric or chronological designation, it should be recorded.
- *Parallel title of series* – transcribe the alternative title if the series has been published in another language or script, following the rules for title proper of the work.
- *ISSN of series* – Although not always the case, a series may have been assigned an ISSN; if so, it should be noted.
- *Subseries* – This is a series within a series.

Note area

Notes are added at the cataloguer's discretion, but their inclusion should follow policy guidelines as laid down by individual organizations. This area is where the cataloguer can record anything they consider noteworthy about the item at hand.

AACR2 1.7 provides explicit guidance on different types of note:

- nature, scope or artistic form
- language of the item and/or translation or adaptation
- source of title proper
- variations in title
- parallel titles and other title information
- statements of responsibility
- edition and history
- material (or type of publication) specific details
- publication, distribution, etc.
- physical description
- accompanying material and supplements
- series
- dissertations
- audience
- reference to published descriptions
- other formats
- summary
- contents

- numbers borne by the item (other than those covered in the standard number area)
- copy being described, library's holdings and restrictions on use
- 'with' notes
- combined notes relating to the original.

This is not actually a comprehensive list: MARC 21 identifies, and has separate fields for, many other types of note. Bear in mind, though, that all of these are optional elements. The purpose of the note area is to provide a location for any information considered important that is not included anywhere else in the description. The amount of detail included will consequently vary considerably from library to library and from cataloguer to cataloguer.

Practice note

It is important to be selective when adding notes to a description, as the lists of types of note can help to identify what information might be useful, but it is easy to include superfluous detail – users don't need to know who made the tea in the recording studio. It is a good idea to establish guidelines on what level of detail is appropriate. It is also important to take care in how notes are expressed: aim for concise and elegant expression. Often the most effective way to express a note is in the form of a quotation taken from the item itself, in which case you enclose the text in quotation marks and, unless it is from the chief source, indicate the source. It is also fine to paraphrase – it doesn't count as plagiarism in this context.

In RDA notes are outlined in the appropriate chapters and relate directly to other elements or fields, for example: Note on Title at **RDA 2.20.2**; Note on Edition Statement at **RDA 2.20.4**; Note on Extent of Item at **RDA 3.22.3**.

This maps more easily onto the MARC formats. Additionally Chapter 7 of RDA, 'Describing content', includes elements that are accommodated in the notes area of AACR2, for example, Supplementary Content at **RDA 7.16** is where information on indexes and bibliography would be recorded, Artistic and/or Technical Credits at **RDA 7.24** is self-explanatory. As in AACR2 it is not a requirement to include this level of detail, local cataloguing policy should establish guidelines.

Standard number and terms of availability
International standard numbers

An ISBN or ISSN should always be included if it is present on the item. It is important to bear in mind that a publisher's number as generally found on CDs and videos is not defined as a standard number in AACR2 so should therefore not be recorded in this area. It can be included as a note. RDA's definition has a broader scope and includes publisher's numbers and other identifiers.

Key-title

The key-title is the 'unique name assigned to a serial by the International Serials Data System (ISDS)'. It is only used for serials and only if an ISSN is present. In RDA this element is, sensibly, located with the other title elements at **RDA 2.3.9**.

Terms of availability

Terms of availability are the price of an item (only if it is printed on the item itself) or, more rarely, other terms by which an item is made available for use, for example, 'Free to members of the society'. In RDA these elements are found in Chapter 4: 'Providing acquisition and access information'.

Conclusion

The ability to identify and record bibliographic elements lies at the heart of cataloguing and is the defining professional skill required by anyone involved in catalogue creation. AACR2 and RDA may differ in their approach, but the bibliographic elements that need to be recorded to identify an individual work are essentially the same in both sets of rules. Entries created with AACR2 are perhaps more elegant and, at first perusal, simpler, at least for those of us familiar with its structure. In fact the more rigid and detailed structure provided by RDA should make the process of catalogue creation more straightforward, and it certainly maps on to the MARC formats more exactly.

4

Access points and headings

What are access points and why do we need them?

When confronted for the first time with the phrase 'access points' you might think that you are being faced with a piece of modern cataloguing jargon. And you might be right.

However, the phrase is indicating the concept of providing structured headings that the catalogue user can predict and, therefore, use to form successful search strategies – search strategies that retrieve the information they are seeking (and ideally *only* the information they are seeking).

In its 'Explanation of Key Terms', **RDA 5.1.4** states, 'The term **access point** refers to a name and/or title, term, code, etc., under which information pertaining to a specific work will be found.'

In other words, an access point is the catalogue user's route into the bibliographic record for the publication (book, CD, website and so on) she is seeking. More specifically, an access point is a specific piece of data that catalogue users can and should expect to provide them with a way into the bibliographic record.

For example, if I am looking for *Jane Eyre*, I expect to be able to search under the title 'Jane Eyre' and find all the records in the catalogue for those books, film and TV adaptations, music scores and so on with the phrase 'Jane Eyre' in their title. In other words, I expect that knowing the title will give me access to the item's record. If I run a search for the title 'Jane Eyre' and nothing is returned, I may assume that the library does not have a copy of that book or film, or any other adaptation of *Jane Eyre*.

'Every reader his book'

This clearly relates the function of access points back to Ranganathan's Laws discussed in Chapter 1:

> Every book its reader.
> Every reader his book.
>
> (Ranganathan, 1957)

In providing access points like title, author(s) and subject, we are essentially predicting the most common ways in which our catalogue users will want to search for an item and ensuring that when they search in these ways they will find the item they are looking for.

Cutter summarized these principles in the first of his 'objects' when he said that the catalogue should:

> enable a person to *find a book* of which either
> the author
> the title
> the subject is known.
>
> (Cutter, 1891)

In the first three of his 'means' he suggested how this type of access might be achieved:

> Author-entry with the necessary references
> Title-entry or title-reference
> Subject-entry, cross references and classed subject-table.
>
> (Cutter, 1891)

Subject access is traditionally the focus of classification and indexing standards, while cataloguing standards such as AACR and RDA have focused on descriptive cataloguing. So beyond noting that it is one of the access points in catalogue records, we are not going to deal with subject entry in this chapter. Instead our interest is in what are often termed 'descriptive access points' or 'bibliographic access points' – Cutter's author-entry and title-entry.

Defining the author

The word 'author' conjures a simple image in our mind – we may think of our favourite author – Jane Austen, perhaps – at work on her novels. Or we might conjure a more generic image of a man at a typewriter or computer screen, or scribbling in a notebook. We will almost certainly think of a single individual creating a single piece of prose.

But then we may think of a range of complications. Are poets 'authors'? What about singer-songwriters or movie producers? What about the editors of collections of essays or letters? What about policy documents issued by government departments and independent strategy units? What about toolkits for teachers or social workers? Can a university be an author? Can a pharmaceutical company?

Cutter (1891) himself recognized that the simple concept of 'authorship' was not straightforward in application. As he put it:

> *Author*, in the narrower sense, is the person who writes a book; in a wider sense,
> it may be applied to him who is the cause of the book's existence by putting
> together the writings of several authors (usually called *the editor*, more properly
> to be called *the collector*). Bodies of men (societies, cities, legislative bodies,
> countries) are to be considered the authors of their memoirs, transactions,
> journals, debates, reports, etc.

Today we would express the idea of 'bodies of men' as 'corporate bodies' (**AACR2 21.B1; RDA 11.0**). RDA also makes prominent the idea of families (**RDA 10.0**). And modern cataloguing standards from the Paris Principles to RDA have made much of the *kind* of responsibility that someone has. Are they an author or an editor? An illustrator or a translator? And if two or more people or organizations are working collaboratively, do they share responsibility for the same things, as when there are two people who write the text, or is there a 'mixed responsibility', as when someone writes the text and someone else draws the illustrations?

Defining the title

Just as they have expanded and expounded on Cutter's basic premise of author-entry, modern cataloguing rules have identified different types of title-entry. As we will see, a title may, straightforwardly, be 'the name of the book given by the author on the title page' (Cutter, 1891), but some books might have several volumes each with a part-title as well as the overall title, and some books and videos might be part of a series, again with their own title and a series title. Some works may be published in different languages and/or might change title slightly over time. We might wish to bring all these incarnations of a work together with some sort of 'uniform title'. Again, the concept of a title is much simpler than the practice.

Access points in the modern catalogue

Lois Mai Chan provides a concise summary of the four types of descriptive access points provided in most modern catalogues:

1   Names of persons who perform certain functions:
   a) Authors
   b) Editors and compilers
   c) Translators
   d) Illustrators
   e) Other related persons (e.g. the addressee of a collection of letters; a person honored by a Festschrift)
2   Names of corporate bodies related to the item being described in a function other than solely as distributor or manufacturer
3   Titles
4   Names of series.

(Chan, 2007)

It should be clear that the first two types in Chan's list are, roughly, an expansion of Cutter's author-entry, while the second two are an expansion of his title-entry.

It is important to realize that different cataloguing and metadata standards have made different decisions on the specifics of dealing with these access points. Although they are all founded on the same principles, outlined above, there are technical variations in:

• selection of access point

- form of heading
- control of headings (often called 'authority control').

In considering how we manage access points in our own catalogues, it is also important to recognize that this is one of the areas of cataloguing strategy that is most frequently affected by systems issues. Clearly, manual and computerized catalogues will work in different ways and present different challenges. Similarly, a modern library management system will almost certainly provide more sophisticated solutions to access point issues than, say, a simple desk-top reference management package or a home-grown Access database.

It should be clear from this that the career cataloguer will encounter local practices and 'workarounds' that vary from catalogue to catalogue. A good cataloguer, and certainly someone capable of managing cataloguing strategy, is able to balance the application of international standards (such as AACR2 and RDA) with local practice to meet their users' needs under the limitations of their cataloguing software. Access points are a key example of the need to be aware of what, exactly, your software does with your data.

The influence of the manual system

The history of AACR, dating back to the 1960s, means that its ways of providing access points were firmly rooted in manual systems. A core concept that this gave rise to was that each item would have a 'main entry' and, where necessary, 'added entries' (cf. **AACR2 21.0A1**) along the lines of Cutter's 'necessary references' discussed above.

In the pre-computer era, creating separate access points was a time-consuming physical process. The classic example is the card catalogue, in which every access point consisted of a physical card with details typed or written on it. Even the simplest work, consisting of a straightforward title and one author, could generate up to ten cards (one for the author, one for the title and one each for up to eight subject headings), all of which had to be written or typed, checked and filed. Any changes would have to be made to each of those ten cards, and if the item was withdrawn from stock, all of those cards would have to be removed.

As a matter of practical time-saving, it made sense to have one main card containing the full catalogue record, and then record briefer details on each of the other cards, with an instruction to the catalogue user to 'see' the main card. Naturally enough, cataloguing rules were established to determine the access point under which this main card should be filed – the 'main entry'. All the other access points for the work were, then 'added entries'.

Computerization of catalogues led to a seismic shift in the means at our disposal to provide catalogue users with access to information. In a modern online catalogue, the creation of an access point is as simple as filling in a field on the database. As John Bowman has put it, 'the cost of providing extra access points is negligible, and all of them act equally as pointers to the same descriptive record' (Bowman, 2007).

Modern attempts to simplify cataloguing practice have bypassed the issues around main and added entries. FRBR, for example, starts by defining different groups of 'entities' and the 'relationship' between them. For example:

> The 'created by' relationship may link a work to a person responsible for the creation of the intellectual or artistic content of the *work*; it may also link a *work* to a *corporate body* responsible for the work. The logical connection between a *work* and a related *person* or *corporate body* serves as the basis both for identifying the *person* or *corporate body* responsible for an individual *work* and for ensuring that all *works* by a particular *person* or *corporate body* are linked to that *person* or *corporate body*.
>
> (FRBR 5.2.2)

A product of the computer-literate 1990s, FRBR's relationships are egalitarian – an access point is an access point is an access point.

Practice note

If you work with a manual system like a card catalogue, you may find it useful to preserve the practice of main entries and added entries.

There have been many calls for the 'FRBRization' of AACR2, and FRBR has had a major impact on RDA. However, the rules relating to access points remain complex – not quite AACR2 and not quite FRBR. In the rest of this chapter, we shall consider specific access points and how the cataloguing standards deal with them.

Personal authors

The most straightforward role that any cataloguer can identify on the title page of a book is that of personal author. As we have seen in the previous chapter on descriptive cataloguing, a personal author appears on the title page with or without the designator 'by':

Essential cataloguing / J.H. Bowman

AACR2 21.1.A1 defines the author as being 'chiefly responsible for the creation of the artistic content of a work'. In the example above, we would provide an access point under the personal name heading for J.H. Bowman, and in following AACR2 this personal name heading would be the main entry.

Of course, there may be more than one author:

Cataloguing / Eric J. Hunter and K.G.B. Bakewell

In this example, we would create access points for both authors. In AACR2, we would consider the first author to be the main entry. In a MARC record, we would enter the personal name heading for Eric J. Hunter in the 100 field. K.G.B. Bakewell would be an added entry in AACR2 terms, and his name heading would be entered in the 700 field in a MARC record.

Under AACR2, the rule of three affects the entries for publications with more than three authors:

Title page: EUROPEAN UNION LAW
TEXT AND MATERIALS
DAMIAN CHALMERS
CHRISTOS HADJIEMMANUIL
GIORGIO MONTI
ADAM TOMKINS

Under AACR2, we would only mention the first author in the statement of responsibility area. What we are really saying is that no single person has made a large enough original contribution to be considered chiefly responsible for this work. So, in AACR2, the main entry would be under title

(European Union Law : text and materials / Damian Chalmers ... [et al.]) and we would make an added entry for the first (and only the first) of the authors, in this case, Chalmers. Hadjiemmanuil, Monti and Tomkins would therefore not appear as access points, so any user searching under one of their names would not find this publication.

In RDA, the rule of three discussed in the last chapter is retained as an option. RDA assumes that the majority of catalogues will contain entries for all four of the contributors, so in this case users searching for any of Chalmers, Hadjiemmanuil, Monti or Tomkins would find this joint work.

Editors

According to AACR2, editors similarly cannot make enough of an original intellectual contribution to a work to be considered 'chiefly responsible' for it. For example:

Sixty women poets / edited by Linda France

In this example, the main entry would be made under title with an added entry under the personal name heading for Linda France.

Sometimes, it may seem to us that an editor has made a significant intellectual contribution to a work. In the example here, Linda France would have selected the poets and poems she included, arranged them within the text and written a small biography of each. She may even have been involved in obtaining the permissions to anthologize the work. Even so, as an editor, according to AACR2 her name cannot be used as the main entry.

Practice note

Managers of some collections make the conscious decision to treat editors as authors. It is a fairly common deviation from AACR2. When you start cataloguing in a new environment, it is always worth checking local practice in the cataloguing notes or manual and by running a search on an edited volume in the catalogue.

Other personal name access points

Authors and editors have clear responsibility for the intellectual content of works but individuals and groups, as identified by Chan (2007), perform other functions that may merit their inclusion as added entry access points. These persons play a greater or lesser part in the realization of a work and so their inclusion as access points is not automatic; it is, to some extent, at the discretion of the cataloguer.

Translators

A translator may have a significant influence on the artistic or intellectual quality of a work, particularly in the case of literary and historical works. In much the same way as a particular conductor of an orchestral piece is deemed to have been responsible for the definitive interpretation of that work, some translations are particularly valued. **AACR2 21.30K1** lists five instances where the name of a translator should be included as an added entry:

  a) the translation is in verse
  or b) the translation is important in its own right
  or c) the work has been translated into the same language more than once
  or d) the wording of the chief source of information of the item being catalogued implies that the translator is the author
  or e) the main entry heading may be difficult for catalogue users to find (e.g. as with many oriental and medieval works).

We would certainly include an added entry access point for Dorothy L. Sayers if we were cataloguing her translation of Dante's *Divine Comedy* because: the translation is in verse, the translation is important in its own right, and the work has been translated into English more than once. We would probably choose not to include an entry for the translator of a Kurt Wallander mystery by Henning Mankell because none of the above instances would apply.

Practice note

It is fairly common for collections to decide to always create an added entry for translators. This decision is made because it can take time to establish

whether or not a translator meets the criteria above, and because even if the translation is the first into a language (**AACR2 21.30K1c**), it may be the first of many. Commonly, cataloguers ask, 'If a new translation is made, do I have to go back and add the translator to the catalogue record for the first translation?' Always giving the translator an added entry simplifies this. When cataloguing in a new environment, this is something to check with local practice.

Illustrators

Even more than is the case with translators, illustrators can make an invaluable contribution to a work. Different editions of an individual title are often judged on the quality of the illustrations. Indeed, some works are valued more for the illustrations than for the text itself. On the other hand, illustrations may be unimportant or an essential but un-creditworthy addition to a text, as in the case of technical drawings. **AACR2 21.30K2** lists three instances where illustrators merit an added entry:

   a) the illustrator's name is given equal or greater prominence in the chief source of information of the item being catalogued to that of the person or corporate body named in the main entry heading
or b)   the illustrations occupy half or more of the item
or c)   the illustrations are considered to be an important feature of the work.

This last instance gives the cataloguer a lot of freedom in deciding whether or not to include an added entry for an illustrator. As is often the case in interpreting cataloguing rules, common sense should prevail. Certainly it would be unthinkable to catalogue A. A. Milne's Winnie the Pooh stories without providing an access point for E. H. Shepherd; equally an access point for Ralph Steadman would always be included in an entry for Hunter S. Thompson's *Fear and loathing in Las Vegas*.

Other related persons

In addition to well defined roles as covered in the previous sections, other individuals or groups may be noted in an added entry if their inclusion would assist catalogue users in locating the works they seek. In general this category of persons includes those who have made no direct intellectual or artistic contribution to the work but whose existence is key to its creation. Instances noted in AACR2 are the addressee of a collection of letters, a person honoured by a Festschrift, and a museum in which an exhibition is held (cf. **21.30F1**)

Instances such as these are rarely encountered, but all eventualities have to be catered for in the rules. Letters are usually collected under their author's name rather than that of their recipient, for example, *Letters of Ted Hughes*, in which case the author would be the main entry heading; or the recipient will be named in the title, for example, *The Dawkins letters*, written by David Robertson to counter Dawkins's *God delusion*. In this latter example main entry would be under David Robertson and it would be appropriate to include an added entry for Richard Dawkins.

Festschriften are compilations of essays gathered to honour a prominent person, usually from the academic sphere. They will be treated as edited works but it is always appropriate to include the name of the person being honoured as an added entry. For example: *Essays on information and libraries: Festschrift in honour of Donald Urquhart* by K.P. Barr and Maurice B. Line. In this example, using AACR2, main entry would be under title, with added entries for Urquhart, Barr and Line.

Corporate bodies

If responsibility for a work is not that of an individual author or a group of persons who have been individually named, then the work may be the creation of a 'corporate body'. For example, 'John Lennon' is a personal name; 'The Beatles' is a corporate body.

The term 'corporate body' covers a very wide range of organizations and groups, including:

- associations
- institutions
- business firms
- non–profit enterprises
- governments
- government agencies
- projects and programmes

- religious bodies
- exhibitions
- expeditions
- fairs
- vessels (ships and spacecraft).

Some of these are obvious and familiar. We have no difficulty in recognizing Microsoft or the Canadian Library Association as corporate bodies. Others are more challenging – when, for example, does something as transient as an event become a corporate body? The answer is: when it has a name.

AACR2 21.1B1 defines a corporate body as: 'an organization or group of persons that is identified by a particular name and that acts, or may act, as an entity'. **RDA 11.0**'s definition is almost identical: 'an organization or group of persons and/or organizations that is identified by a particular name and that acts, or may act, as a unit'. Both definitions stress that a corporate body has to be identified by a 'particular name'. The easiest way to identify a name is to check whether the initial letters of words are consistently capitalized. Internet Librarian 2010 is, therefore, a corporate body, as is The Big Chill. So, although diverse, corporate bodies are usually easily identifiable (they are named and they are not persons).

The rules for creation of access points for corporate bodies are essentially the same as for works of personal authorship – they depend on the role of the body in the realization of the work. Under **AACR2 21.1B2**, the name of a corporate body can be the main entry point or can be included as an added entry, and AACR2 gives detailed instructions to assist in determining whether the name of the body would be the main entry heading.

The name of a corporate body would be a main entry access point if the work being catalogued falls into one or more of the following categories:

- those of an administrative nature dealing with the corporate body itself, including policies, members and resources
- some legal, governmental and religious works, including laws, decrees, regulations, constitutions, court rules, treaties, court decisions, legislative hearings, religious laws and liturgical works
- those that record the collective thought of the body, including reports of commissions and committees, position statements

- those that report the collective activity of a conference (e.g. proceedings), an expedition, or an event falling within the definition of a corporate body provided that the conference, expedition or event is prominently named in the item
- those that result from the collective activity of a performing group where the responsibility of the group goes beyond that of mere performance (with the exception of some sound recordings where the name of a group of performers can be a main entry heading, see **AACR2 21.23**)
- cartographic materials emanating from a corporate body.

This may seem complicated, but in reality it is not. Examining the rules in abstract terms is one thing; interpreting them when we have an item in front of us that needs to be catalogued is another. It is usually obvious when a corporate body has performed a role in a work's creation that merits a main entry access point.

Name authority control

Anyone who has ever Googled themselves (and a 2008 study by Pew Internet (Madden, 2008) found that 47% of internet-users in the USA have searched for information about themselves online) will have come across the phenomenon of uncontrolled name entry. Certain websites exist that claim to aggregate information about an individual, which, through a phrase search on the name, form a composite persona made up of the characteristics and contact details of everyone with that name.

On such web pages, 'Anne Welsh' is not only a lecturer in LIS with a background in cataloguing and special collections, and a hobby writing poetry. 'She' is also a social worker in the south west of England, a paediatrician in the USA, a lecturer in Education in Scotland and a hairdresser, among other things. Some of these are more believable combinations than others – it is entirely plausible that someone who worked as an information officer at a drugs charity might have been (or might go on to become) a social worker, for example.

Name Authority Control aims to unpick just such confusions, and to establish a single 'bibliographic identity' for each person who has contributed to a publication on our catalogue. In doing so, we differentiate the thousands of John Smiths or, to take an example closer to home, the authors on

ophthalmology, chemistry, taxation and property from the author on cataloguing whose name appears in a search for 'j h bowman' on Google Scholar.

The J. H. Bowman who interests us as cataloguers has pointed out:

> Authority control is not mentioned specifically in AACR2, but it is implied in the
> sections dealing with forms of name. It is the process whereby a library or
> cataloguing agency establishes authorized forms of name for *access points* and
> ensures that they are used consistently for all occurrences of such names.
>
> (Bowman, 2007)

Thinking back to Cutter's 'objects' we can remember that the first way in
which he suggests someone should be able to find a book is by author.
Similarly, he instructs that from the library's perspective, demonstrating what
it has 'by a given author' is the primary object – before even demonstrating
what it has 'on a given subject'. In the language of FRBR, we want to be able
to collocate the library's holdings by an author.

On a practical level, we might say that these are our objectives:

- All relevant items have an entry under the *same form* of the heading:
  - The same person with different name forms has only one heading.
  - Different people with the same name have different headings.
- Cross-references are made consistently.
- Updates to headings need only be made once – to the authority record.

Achieving authority control in practice

The method of authority control is to some degree dependent on the kind of
system the catalogue uses. Some library management systems have very
sophisticated authority control modules, linked to the bibliographic records
in such a way that when the authorized name form is changed in the authority
record, this automatically changes the appearance of the name in every
bibliographic record in which it appears – often this change occurs during the
catalogue's overnight processing.

In library management systems without an authority control module, or
validation list that will automatically update individual catalogue records,
we would at least expect to be able to run a 'batch modify' operation to update

the name entry for an author whose name had changed. In some libraries, cataloguers might be authorized to perform such operations; in others, it might be necessary to request the systems librarian to do this.

In a card catalogue, a physical movement of cards is often involved. If an author called Jane Smith changed her name to Jane Brown, in order to keep all her books together, rather than having her earlier books under 'Smith, Jane' and her later books under 'Brown, Jane', we would move all the cards for 'Smith, Jane' to 'Brown, Jane'. If we had the time and the resources, we might retype the cards so they all showed 'Brown, Jane'. If we did not, we might score through 'Smith' and write 'Brown' above it neatly. If we had even less time (or we had hundreds of cards headed 'Smith, Jane'), we might make a guide card (the ones with tabs that stick up above the general cards to guide the user in a card drawer) headed 'Brown, Jane' and type on it 'Until 2011, Jane Brown published as Jane Smith'. There are examples of some card catalogues where the cards are left in their separate 'Brown' and 'Smith' locations, with see also references from one to the other, but this is really saving the time of the cataloguer at the expense of the time of the reader, which, of course, is contrary to Ranganathan's laws.

In all of these operations it is important to be able to distinguish which form of name to use as the access point for the record. AACR2 rules 22 and 24 instruct us how to form headings for persons and corporate bodies, respectively, but before we look at some examples, let us continue to explore the workflow of authority control in a cataloguing department.

Sources for authority control

The Name Authority Cooperative Program (NACO) of the Program for Cooperative Cataloguing is the international co-operative programme for authority control. Major libraries around the world contribute authority records in return for access to the data, held on servers at the Library of Congress (NACO, 2011). If you work in a library that participates in NACO, you will have access to the NACO Name Authority Files (NAF), and will be expected to check these for the correct form of each personal and corporate name you enter as an access point in your records.

The Library of Congress provides a free database of NAF at http://authorities.loc.gov so any library, of whatever scale, can incorporate authority control into their cataloguing process, as long as they have an internet connection.

Practice note

Libraries employing paraprofessionals for basic catalogue entry vary in the stage at which authority control is employed. Sometimes students express outrage that the library in which they worked pre-library school 'did not use the Library of Congress NAF', but further investigation, by student or lecturer, usually turns up a level of authority control being carried out by a senior member of staff at the library concerned, often monthly, and always referring to the Library of Congress NAF. It is very rare for a library not to make use of this free service, as it is obviously quicker to look names up on a preprepared database than to construct the name headings independently in-house.

Sometimes names or corporate bodies – especially conferences – do not make it onto the Library of Congress NAF before you have a copy of a publication for which you need a heading. This is particularly true of names and organizations of particular relevance to a region outside the USA, and there are cases where a heading is simply never created. Remember, these are the *Library of Congress*'s authority files, and ask yourself how high priority an anthology by an English regional writing group or a DVD by an Australian local youth theatre is likely to be in the cataloguing shelves of that institution – if they ever get there.

Other reference sources can be useful for establishing names that are not available on the Library of Congress NAF (or not available there yet) – for example, national bibliographies, dictionaries of national biography and subject-specific directories.

Using the Library of Congress Name Authority Files

When using the Library of Congress NAF for the first time, it is important to be clear in your mind that the records are structured according to the MARC 21 Format for Authority Data (Library of Congress Network Development and MARC Standards Office, 2009). Although closely related to the MARC 21 Format for Bibliographic Data, it is *not the same format*:

The *MARC 21 Format for Authority Data* is designed to be a carrier for information concerning the authorized forms of names, subjects, and subject subdivisions to be used in constructing access points in MARC records, the forms of these names, subjects and subject subdivisions that should be used as references to the authorized forms, and the interrelationships among these forms. A **name** may be used as a main, added, series, or subject access entry.

(MARC 21, 2010) (emphasis in the original)

Personal names appear as X00 and corporate bodies appear as X10. There are also files for conference headings at X11. The specific types of cross-references and linking are the same across these three areas, so if you understand how one works, you can apply the principles to the other two areas.

Let us use the X00 area for personal names as our example.

Within this area there are three important features that help us to navigate the NAF and create our own authority files:

100 – Heading – Personal Name (NR [Non-Repeatable field])
400 – See From Tracing – Personal Name (R [Repeatable field])
500 – See Also From Tracing – Personal Name (R)

Here we have another piece of cataloguer jargon. A 'tracing' is a cross-reference specific to authority files. This is a hangover from the days of the card catalogue, when the main entry card contained, usually on its back, a list of all the other places entries were filed. In this way, if you ever had to remove that card, or change it, you could trace your way back through the catalogue to each of them. For practical purposes, you can think of a tracing as a cross-reference.

If you are familiar with subject cataloguing, or, indeed, have used a book index, you will be familiar with the idea of 'see' and 'see also'. Wherever you come across a 'see' reference it means 'don't use this heading, *see* this one and use it instead'. Wherever you come across a 'see also' reference it means 'you might want to use this heading, but you might want to *see also* this other heading and use it too'. In MARC authority format, wherever you see a 400 it means see, and wherever you see a 500 it means see also.

This can be hard to imagine in the abstract: beginning cataloguers often struggle to visualize a reason for not having everything by the same person under the same heading.

International bestselling crime novelist Agatha Christie provides us with a fine example. If we search the Library of Congress NAF for 'Christie, Agatha' we find the authorized heading for her. The summary screen contains this information:

Heading (1XX)	Christie, Agatha, 1890-1976
Search Also Under (5XX)	Mallowan, Agatha Christie, 1890-1976
Search Also Under (5XX)	Westmacott, Mary, 1890-1976

Each heading underlined on the display screen forms a hypertext link that takes us to an authorized heading. Students often ask 'How can one woman have three different headings?' The answer is that although Agatha Christie was *one person* she chose to write under *three different names* each of which represented a different *bibliographic identity*:

- Agatha Christie, the best known bibliographic identity, was used for crime novels.
- Mary Westmacott was a bibliographic identity used for novels with a supernatural edge.
- Agatha Christie Mallowan was a bibliographic identity used for publications concerned with the archaeological digs on which she accompanied her husband.

We can imagine that a user who was writing a comprehensive bibliography or a biography of the *person* Agatha Christie would have an interest in all of her works produced under all of her *bibliographic identities*.

Someone interested only in the supernatural stories might not appreciate having to trawl through lots of murder mysteries to find what they are looking for, so the separate bibliographic identity Mary Westmacott provides a useful access point to just the books Christie chose to write under that name.

Similarly, someone looking for archaeological material wouldn't want to sift out all the murder mysteries – and a murder-mystery fan might be a bit disappointed to retrieve a pamphlet about archaeological finds instead of a crime novel, so the Agatha Christie Mallowan bibliographic identity comes into its own.

From the summary record, if we click through the heading for 'Christie,

Agatha, 1890-1976' we can see the authorized heading and 'see also' tracings:

100 1_$a Christie, Agatha, **|d**1890-1976

500 1_$a Mallowan, Agatha Christie, **|d**1890-1976
500 1_$a Westmacott, Mary, **|d**1890-1976

From the summary record, clicking through 'Mallowan, Agatha Christie, 1890-1976' we can see the authorized heading and 'see also' tracings:

100 1_$a Mallowan, Agatha Christie, **|d**1890-1976

500 1_$a Christie, Agatha, **|d**1890-1976
500 1_$a Westmacott, Mary, **|d**1890-1976

Finally, if we go back to the summary record again and click through 'Westmacott, Mary, 1890-1976' we see the authorized heading and 'see also' tracings:

100 1_$a Westmacott, Mary, **|d**1890-1976

500 1_$a Christie, Agatha, **|d**1890-1976
500 1_$a Mallowan, Agatha Christie, **|d**1890-1976

So we can see how these three authority records relate to each other.

If we go back to the full record for 'Christie, Agatha, 1890-1976', we can also pick out the 'see' references, given as 400s:

100 1_$a Christie, Agatha, **|d**1890-1976

400 1_$a Christie, Agatha Miller, **|d**1890-1976
400 1_$a Christie, Agatha Mary Clarissa Miller,**|d**1890-1976
400 1_$a Kri-xta, A-ga-ta,**|d**1890-1976
400 1_$a Christie, Agata,**|d**1890-1976
400 1_$a Kristi, Agata,**|d**1890-1976

All of these see references represent names under which Christie is known, and under which she might be sought, but which are not authorized as headings. Some library management systems can do clever things with data like this – so if someone searches under 'Kristi, Agata', for example, they may be taken straight to records for publications with the heading 'Christie, Agatha, 1890-1976'. Whether your library management system is capable of this type of sophistication or not, as a cataloguer you enter books under the authorized version, not one of those in the 400 see references.

There are many other features of this MARC authority record. If you are interested, explore further in the manual for MARC 21 Format for Authority Records online. For practical, day-to-day purposes, we are only going to look at one more field in this record: 670 Source data found.

670   Source data found

This repeatable field is used by the cataloguers who have created and updated the authority record to store information about where they have found information about this bibliographic identity. In our record for Agatha Christie, there are sources for her name in English and in other languages, including:

100 1_$a Christie, Agatha, **|d**1890-1976

670 __$a Her The mysterious affair at Styles, 1920.
670 __$a Fitzgibbon, R.H. The Agatha Christie companion, c1980:**|b**t.p. (Agatha Christie) p.15 (b. 9/15/90)
670 __$aNUC pre-56**|b**(hdg: Christie, Agatha Miller, 1891-; usage: Agatha Christie; Agatha Christie Mallowan; Mary Westmacott; full name: Agatha Mary Clarissa Miller Christie)

These three sources tell us that, among other sources, the cataloguer(s) consulted one of Christie's own novels; a reference work about Christie; and an old national union catalogue.

Practice note

When Wikipedia first launched, there was debate in the cataloguing community about its appropriateness or otherwise as a source for authority control work. We now see it frequently in Library of Congress Name Authority Files, so assume that this debate is over.

Forming name headings

This brings us to a brief introduction to how name headings are formed. Earlier on in the chapter we discussed when a personal name or a corporate body merits an access point (under AACR2). Once we have decided to make an entry, we consult the Name Authority Files (NACO if we have access to them, or the free Library of Congress ones otherwise), where, for most modern publications we can expect to find the appropriate heading to use.

Sometimes we will not find the heading we need on the name authority files and will have to create our own headings, and in this we are guided by **AACR2 22** for headings for persons and **AACR2 24** for headings for corporate bodies.

AACR2 22.1A instructs us:

> In general, choose... the name by which he or she is commonly known. This may be the person's real name, pseudonym, title of nobility, nickname, initials, or other appellation...
>
> e.g.   William Shakespeare
>   Capability Brown not Lancelot Brown
>   John Julius Norwich not Viscount Norwich

AACR2 22.1B goes on:

> Determine the name by which a person is commonly known from the chief source of information... of works by that person issued in his or her language. If the person... is not known primarily as an author, determine the name... from reference sources...

If we think of the 670 notes in our authority record for Agatha Christie, we can understand how the cataloguer(s) who created it arrived at the particular form of Christie's name to form the authorized heading for her crime novels.

AACR2 also sets out the order in which names should be entered, which is then followed by MARC:

> **AACR2 22.4A** If a person's name... consists of several parts, select... that part of the name under which the person would normally be listed in authoritative alphabetic lists... If, however, a person's preference is known to be different from the normal usage, follow that preference.

> **22.5A1** Enter a name containing a surname... under that surname unless subsequent rules (e.g. **22.6** [nobility], **22.10** [initials, letters, numerals], **22.28** [Thai names]) provide for entry under a different element

Again, thinking of Agatha Christie, these rules explain the ordering of her name, surname followed by forename – 'Christie, Agatha'.

An increasingly common name form in English is the compound surname, which is covered in **AACR2 22.5C**:

> **22.5C2** Preferred... name known. Enter... under the element by which the person... prefers to be entered. If this is unknown, enter... under which it is listed in reference sources...

> **22.5C3** Hyphenated surnames. If the elements... are regularly... hyphenated, enter under the first element.

We can see these rules in action in the Library of Congress NAF in the record for the artist Charles Rennie Mackintosh:

100 1_$aMackintosh, Charles Rennie, |d1868-1928

670 __$aHowarth T.|bCharles Rennie Mackintosh, 1952
670 __$aC.R. Mackintosh, architectural drawings, 1990|bt.p. (C.R. Mackintosh)

These two publications have been consulted in the preparation of the heading, showing that while Mackintosh's name often appears in full, it has appeared in the format [forename initials] [surname], indicating that Mackintosh is his surname and should therefore be the entry element.

Of course, people use many different formats for their names from the ones explored here. People may use only one name (like Plato or Madonna), or may have a title (like Sir Walter Scott or Princess Diana). They may even prefer to write under their initials only (like H.D.). AACR2 caters for all these variations and many more. The best advice is if you have a name that doesn't consist of a forename and a surname, and it doesn't appear in the name authority files, consult AACR2, bearing in mind that the name may:

- include a prefix (e.g. Walter de la Mare), in which case the nationality of the person affects the format, as discussed in **AACR2 22.5D**
- include a title, in which case it depends largely on whether they are commonly known by the title or not, and whether a surname is included as well as the title or not, as discussed in **AACR2 22.6** and **AACR2 22.12**
- include a patronymic (e.g. Isaac ben Aaron), in which case it is entered in direct order (Isaac ben Aaron) and not inverted, **AACR2 22.8B**
- include the name of a royal house (e.g. Louis Bonaparte), in which case it is entered in direct order (Louis Bonaparte), **AACR2 22.8C**
- consist only of initials (e.g. H.D.), in which case it is entered as initials under **AACR2 22.10**
- refer to a saint, in which case **AACR2 22.13A** instructs us to 'Add *Saint*... unless the person was a pope, emperor, empress, king, or queen, in which case follow **22.16A-22.16B**' and **AACR2 22.13B** tells us to 'Add any other suitable word or phrase necessary to distinguish between two saints' and gives us the examples 'Augustine, *Saint, Archbishop of Canterbury*' and 'Augustine, *Saint, Bishop of Hippo*'.

One key thing to notice in current practice in establishing name headings concerns the use of dates. AACR2 suggests the use of dates only in the case of distinguishing between two people with the same name:

> **AACR2 22.17A** Add a person's dates (birth, death, etc.)... as the last element of a heading if the heading is otherwise identical to another...
> *Optionally*, add date(s) to any personal name, even if there is no need to distinguish between headings.

Although the addition of dates is only an option in AACR2, we have already seen that examples from the Library of Congress Name Authority File were unique name forms which (as at 2012) include dates:

100 1_$aChristie, Agatha, **$d**1890-1976
100 1_$aMackintosh, Charles Rennie, **$d**1868-1928

Practice note

From the point of view of managing workflow, it makes sense to add dates when you establish the name heading, as you will already be consulting reference sources, which often include dates. Otherwise when a second person comes along with the same name, you have to create a name heading including dates for that person and look up the dates of the first person in order to distinguish them in an equitable manner.

Headings for corporate bodies

In our discussion of authority control, we said that the principle for corporate bodies was the same as for personal names. Authority records for corporate bodies display with the authorized heading in the 110 field, with 'see' tracings at 410 and 'see also' tracings at 510. They also contain 670 fields, which include the sources consulted in forming the headings.

Increasingly, the 670 field in corporate bodies' authority records refers to the organization's website(s), as in this example:

110 2_$aJoint Steering Committee for Development of RDA

510 2_$aJoint Steering Committee for Revision of AACR

670 __$aJoint Steering Committee for Development of RDA WWW Home page, Oct. 26, 2007: **$b**(Joint Steering Committee for Development of RDA; new name of the Joint Steering Committee for Revision of AACR)

Here, the cataloguer has referred to the JSC's website to extract this information, then created a new heading for the new form of the name, with 'see also' references between the old form and the new.

The rules in AACR2 that describe how to create headings for corporate bodies (**AACR2 24**) are just as extensive as those for personal names, and again, the general advice is if you cannot find an entry for the organization you need to enter in the name authority files, consult AACR2 to find the correct format.

This idea is stated explicitly in the general rule:

> **AACR2 24.1A** General rule. Enter a corporate body under the name by which it is commonly identified, except when the rules that follow provide for entering it under the name of a higher or related body (see **24.13**) or under the name of a government (see **24.18**).

Most corporate bodies are entered just as they appear:

American Library Association
University of Sydney
United Nations

Where a corporate body is part of a larger organization, **AACR2 24.13** instructs us to give the larger organization first, then the smaller one. There are different types of subordination set out in AACR2, but the form of heading follows the same principle:

Canadian Library Association. Committee on Canadian Subject Headings
King's College London. Centre for Computing in the Humanities

Government agencies may also be entered as subordinates, as set out at **AACR2 24.18**. Again, there are different types of government agency, but the principle followed is largely the same.

Even when you become really experienced in creating these headings, it is *always* worth checking AACR2 and the Library of Congress authority records, not least because there can be important disagreements between the two:

AACR2 24.18A TYPE 5 United Kingdom. Home Office
Library of Congress NAF 110 1_$a Great Britain.$bHome Office

AACR2 24.18A TYPE 5 United Kingdom. Ministry of Defence
Library of Congress NAF 110 1_$a Great Britain.$bMinistry of Defence

Practice note

If you work in a collection with papers from UK government departments and agencies, check whether you follow the Library of Congress or AACR2 for the name of the nation-state.

Similarly, the abbreviation 'Dept.' appears in many Library of Congress records, including:

110 1_$aVermont.$bDept. of Water Resources

which is given in **AACR2 24.18A** TYPE 1 as

Vermont. Department of Water Resources

RDA explicitly plans to return to the use of 'Department' as part of its sweeping aside of abbreviations.

It is worth being aware that there are special rules in AACR2 for many forms of corporate body, including:

- religious orders and societies (e.g. Franciscans), **AACR2 24.3D1**
- government officials (e.g. United States. President), **AACR2 24.20**
- legislative bodies (e.g. United States. Congress. House of Representatives), **AACR2 24.21**
- armed forces (e.g. Canada. Canadian Armed Forces), **AACR2 24.24**
- religious bodies and officials, **AACR2 24.27**.

AACR2 24.4 instructs certain additions to be made to clarify certain corporate bodies' headings. Of particular note is the instruction at **24.4B1** to add a designator when a 'name alone does not convey the idea of a corporate body'. Students are always surprised that ships and spacecraft are corporate bodies:

Apollo 11 (Spacecraft)

Bounty (Ship)

Similarly:

Google (Firm)
Facebook (Firm)

Titles

In addition to the author another aspect of a work that can generate a main entry heading is its title. **RDA 6.2.1.1** defines a title as: 'a word, phrase, character, or group of characters by which a work is known'. What AACR2 terms the 'title proper' is the title of the work as it appears in the chief source of information, e.g. on the title page of a book. In works of personal or corporate body authorship, as discussed in the preceding sections, the title of the work would generate an added entry, but there are occasions where the title becomes the main entry point. **AACR2 21.1C1** lists four instances where this applies:

> a) the personal authorship is unknown or diffuse [more than three persons or corporate bodies]
>
> *or* b) it is a collection of works by different persons or bodies [i.e., edited works]
>
> *or* c) it emanates from a corporate body but does not fall into any of the categories given in 21.1B2 [outlined above] and is not of personal authorship
>
> *or* d) it is accepted as sacred scripture by a religious group.

In the first three instances noted here, no single person or body is deemed to have made a large enough contribution to the intellectual or artistic content of the work to merit a main entry heading; the title of the work becomes the main entry. In the final instance, even though we may be able to identify an author AACR2 dictates that main entry must be under title. For example if cataloguing: The gospel according to St. Luke/by St. Luke, the main entry would be under title with an added entry for Luke, *Saint*.

Collective title

The majority of works with a collective title fall under the category of edited works, which we have already covered: main entry is under title, with added entries for up to three editors. In some cases a collection of works by different persons or bodies lacks a collective title; in this case treatment is different. For example:

> A journey to the Western Islands of Scotland / Samuel Johnson. The journal of a tour to the Hebrides / James Boswell ; [both] edited with an introduction and notes by Peter Levy

In this example the main entry would be the first named author, Johnson, with added entries for Boswell, Levy and both titles.

Uniform and preferred titles

Reference has already been made to the 'title proper' of a work; this is not necessarily the only form of title that generates an entry point in the catalogue. In AACR we find the concept of the 'uniform title'; the equivalent in RDA is the 'preferred title'. Here, for brevity's sake, the term uniform title will be used to explain and illustrate the concept. Following the general rules for entry under title, a uniform title can be either a main or added entry heading.

The need for a uniform title arises as a consequence of the major function of the catalogue: to assist users in finding the items they are searching for. A uniform title brings together all manifestations and editions of a work that may have appeared under various titles. This would perhaps include translations of works from other languages, variations in the title of different editions of a work, and works in which the popularly known title varies from the title proper.

In the case of a translated work the uniform title would comprise the title in the original language followed by the language of the translation:

> Title proper: The tin drum
> Uniform title: Blechtrommel. English

This form of uniform title is useful in collections that include a large amount of foreign literature where users may want to read works in the original language as well as in translation. It would not be useful if the majority of the collection is in the English language.

In the case of variations in title, some works will have been published many times with many different versions of the title appearing as the title proper. Bowman's (2007) example, Hamlet, illustrates this very effectively:

The first quarto edition of Shakespeare's Hamlet
Hamlet
Hamlet, Prince of Denmark
Shakespeare's Hamlet
The tragedie of Hamlet, Prince of Denmark
The tragedy of Hamlet
The tragicall historie of Hamlet Prince of Denmarke
William Shakespeare's Hamlet

All these titles refer to the same work and so it is obviously useful to bring all the various editions of that work together under a uniform title: Hamlet.

Another example of this can be found in the titles of works in the English language published in the USA or Australia, for example, which may differ from the title of the UK edition. In this case the title of the edition published in the home country of the cataloguing agency would be used as the uniform title. For cataloguing agencies in the UK:

Title proper: Harry Potter and the sorcerer's stone (U.S. edition)
Uniform title: Harry Potter and the philosopher's stone (U.K. edition)

This often also applies to films (as in the Harry Potter example when the book and film had different titles). On some occasions the two titles are similar enough to be retrieved in a search of the catalogue, a title search for 'Harry Potter' would retrieve both versions of the above example. This is, of course, not always the case:

Title proper: Conqueror worm (U.S. title)
Uniform title: Witchfinder General (U.K. title)

Again dependent on the number of items affected, if the collection includes books and other media with variant titles, it is useful to create a uniform title to bring all these versions together in the catalogue.

The most common use of uniform titles, and one which is always to be recommended, is to collocate works in which the original title or title proper is not in common usage. This applies to many classic works of literature including works of Shakespeare (as in the Hamlet example) and Dickens:

Title proper:	The posthumous papers of the Pickwick Club
Uniform title:	Pickwick papers

Even in our era of keyword and phrase searching, it is clear that the uniform title Pickwick papers will assist the user in finding the item – a phrase search for 'Pickwick Papers' surrounded by quotation marks would not find 'The posthumous papers of the Pickwick Club' since 'papers' appears several words before 'Pickwick'.

Another use of uniform title is to collocate the collected works of a single author. It is obviously desirable to separate collections of works from individual titles by an author both in the catalogue and on the library shelves. As Bowman (2007) points out, AACR2's treatment of this is inadequate as no mention is made of the purpose of the collective title in this context: it is to ensure that the collected works of an author will be filed before individual works. The uniform title for collected works consists of a term describing the nature of the collection (cf. **AACR2 25.8, 25.9, 25.10**):

Works:	for the complete works of an author
Selections:	for the selected works of an author
Specific forms:	Correspondence
	Essays
	Novels
	Plays
	Poems
	Prose works
	Short stories
	Speeches

In all cases the main entry is under author with added entries for the uniform title and the title proper of the collection:

Main entry: Shakespeare, William
Added entry: Works
Added entry: Complete works of William Shakespeare

Main entry: Chopin, Frederic
Added entry: Selections
Added entry: Selected works for piano

Main entry: Beckett, Samuel
Added entry: Plays
Added entry: Complete dramatic works of Samuel Beckett

Main entry: Sayers, Dorothy L.
Added entry: Short stories
Added entry: Complete stories

It is important to emphasize, as is hopefully made clear in the above examples, that the inclusion of uniform titles in a catalogue is not mandatory in the rules as laid down in **AACR2 25.1A** but at the cataloguer's discretion. An entry under uniform title may be created, depending on:

- how well the work is known
- how many manifestations of the work are involved
- whether another work with the same title proper has been identified
- whether the main entry is under title
- whether the work was originally in another language
- the extent to which the catalogue is used for research purposes.

Using these guidelines, if the aim is to assist users, which it is, then the catalogues of most collections would require some access points under uniform title, certainly in the case of titles in common usage differing from the title proper. Of course instances like these will be rare; the vast majority of the collection will not require such access points.

In **RDA 6.2.2.4** the concept of a preferred title replaces that of the uniform title:

> For works created after 1500, choose as the preferred title the title in the original language by which the work has become known through use in resources embodying the work or in reference sources.

> For works created before 1501, choose the title or form of title in the original language by which the work is identified in modern sources.

Although the wording is almost identical to that of AACR, RDA takes a more user-centred approach in that the preferred title is a core element in identifying a work: the popular title or title in common usage is preferred over the 'title proper'. In fact the concepts of the title proper and the uniform title as access points, as established in AACR, are largely absent in RDA. RDA retains the 'title proper' in the description element and caters for other forms of title in its inclusion of the optional 'Variant Titles' element, which is a form of title that differs from the chosen preferred title. In an example looked at above:

Preferred title: Pickwick papers
Variant title: The posthumous papers of the Pickwick Club

It is left to the cataloguer's discretion whether or not to include the 'title proper' as a variant title entry point.

Multipart works and series

A single work may be published in several volumes or a series of individual works by one or more authors may be published as part of a series. It is usually easy to distinguish one from the other but it is useful to clarify the terms. A multipart work is defined in **AACR2 Appendix D** as: 'a monograph complete, or intended to be completed, in a finite number of separate parts'.

It is possible to distinguish between a single work published in several volumes, e.g. Macaulay's History of England, Encyclopaedia Britannica, and several works published in a single series, e.g. the diverse works published in the Penguin Classics series. In the context of choice of access points their treatment is straightforward.

A work by a single author would have main entry under the name of the author (a person or a corporate body) with added entry under title including volume or part number:

Main entry:	Macaulay, Thomas Babington
Added entry:	History of England from the accession of James II: Vol. 6

A multipart work by multiple authors would have main entry under the title and possibly an added entry or entries under editor(s) or compiler(s):

Main entry:	Encyclopaedia Britannica
Main entry:	Oxford English dictionary
Added entry:	Simpson, John
Added entry:	Weiner, Edmund

When cataloguing multipart works like encyclopedias, dictionaries and directories it is certainly not recommended that a separate catalogue entry should be created for each volume. A single entry is all that is required; the number of volumes in the set can be noted in the physical description field.

A work that is part of a series would have main entry under author (or title if it is an edited work) with an added entry for the name of the series:

Main entry:	Dickens, Charles
Added entry:	Little Dorrit
Added entry:	Penguin Classics

This helps to distinguish between different versions of the same work:

Main entry:	Dickens, Charles
Added entry:	Little Dorrit
Added entry:	Wordsworth Classics

There are several examples of series in Chapter 10:

- *Noble deeds of the world's heroines* is part of the Brave deeds series
- *The essays of Michel de Montaigne Volume II* is part of Bohn's Standard Library
- *Provenance research in book history* is part of British Library Studies in the History of the Book.

As you can see from their MARC records, there are two fields within MARC that are used, the 490 *Series statement* and the 830 *Series added entry*.

What this means, essentially, is that when we are dealing with a series, we need to make an entry in both fields.

This system of dealing with series in MARC was introduced in 2009, so be aware that you may see older records on your catalogue (and other libraries' catalogues) that contain older tags (the superseded 440 tag, for example).

Under the old system, time was spent deciding whether the series was being entered solely for description, or if it was an entry point, and we used different fields according to this decision. MARC now deals with this using the first indicator of the 490 field:

First indicator 0 – series not traced
First indicator 1 – series traced

Cataloguers / libraries who make use of this distinction argue that some series are not titles under which users would search. Examples offered tend to be the Penguin Classics or Oxford World's Classics series. Other cataloguers argue that any series may be a search term for a user. Certainly, there are book historians and collectors who are interested in series, and the introduction or other critical apparatus of a particular series may be important.

We would recommend always tracing series, and always creating a series added entry.

Practice Note

Some Library Management Systems are capable of generating an 830 entry from the 490, so check whether you need to enter the 830 manually.

5

RDA: resource description and access

This chapter covers the history of the new code, picks up on some of the changes indicated elsewhere in the book, and finally offers practical advice for libraries and other cataloguing agencies considering if, how and when they should make the change from AACR2 to RDA.

Timeline to change

Let us start with the simplest narrative – the administrative history of the new code. The history of RDA is outlined on the Joint Steering Committee (JSC) website at www.rda-jsc.org/rda.html#background, and referenced in most publications on the new code, including Chris Oliver's recent book *Introducing RDA: a guide to the basics* (Oliver, 2010).

RDA grew out of the process begun in 2004 to produce the next edition of the *Anglo-American Cataloguing Rules*. Following the circulation of the draft of the first part of AACR3, it was decided in 2005 that a new approach was needed, and work began under the title *RDA: resource description and access*.

Between 2005 and 2009 various drafts of the new code were circulated for constituency review, and members of the cataloguing community around the world offered feedback and opinions.

A key shift between AACR2 and RDA is the new code's conception as a digital product. In June 2010, the RDA Toolkit was presented to the world, with a free trial period of just over three months. Later in 2010, a paper version of RDA was published, in response to demands from the community, and particularly from smaller institutions which could not afford the annual subscription to the online product. However, throughout the process, the JSC has stressed that RDA is not a paper product, and full understanding (and updates) is available only through the online version.

One impact of the transparency of the processes around the creation of the new code is an awareness on the part of the worldwide cataloguing community that it has not yet been decided when the major Anglo-American cataloguing agencies – the Library of Congress and the British Library, will adopt the code. Because the processes preparing for previous codes were more closed, the average cataloguer in the stacks did not feel the need to engage with them until the Library of Congress and the British Library were beginning to implement them.

This time round, we have been able to follow the US tests, run through the national libraries and over 20 other test centres, selected from applicants across the country. Documentation and training materials have been made available at www.loc.gov/catdir/cpso/RDAtest/rdatest.html and these, along with the print and online versions of RDA itself and a plethora of articles and books, have enabled any cataloguer, anywhere, to keep up with changes.

In June 2011, the US national libraries announced that they will 'adopt RDA with certain conditions and that implementation will not occur before January 1, 2013' (Library of Congress, National Agricultural Library and National Library of Medicine, 2011).

Changes

The JSC has been at pains to point out that changes from AACR2 to RDA have been kept to a minimum, and an attempt has been made to ensure that most changes could be implemented retrospectively using a batch modification to existing catalogue records.

However, some decisions, such as the relegation of the rule of three to an option, would require manual input *if* they were to be implemented retrospectively.

The main cataloguing e-mail lists AUTOCAT and RDA-L have highlighted the natural cataloguer's wariness for any change that introduces inconsistency to their catalogue. After all, we are taught on day one of cataloguing at library school that consistency is the quality prized above all others in a catalogue, and the feature which renders search and retrieval predictable for the user. We do not like interruptions to that predictability.

That said, there can be few of us who work on catalogues so new that they were created entirely under AACR2. Most catalogues are already hybrid, containing records created under AACR, and, in some cases, earlier codes. The British Library still contains a proportion of records created under Panizzi's Rules.

Certainly, when AACR2 was introduced, batch modifications altered some fields within records to be AACR2 compliant, while other aspects (Name Authority pre-1967, anyone?) had to be updated with each individual case, as records surfaced that could be updated alongside the creation of, say, a new edition, or a new book by the same author.

Some of the major changes have already been adopted by the MARBI committee and implemented in MARC 21. The MARC standards website contains a section called RDA in MARC at www.loc.gov/marc/ RDAinMARC29.html and this is regularly updated.

So, already we can see there is capacity to move away from AACR2's reliance on general material designators and instead use RDA's Content Type (MARC 336), Media Type (MARC 337) and Carrier Type (MARC 338).

If we were creating RDA records for the examples at the end of this book, they would each have the following content, media and carrier type entries:

336	$atext
	$btxt
	$2rdacontent
337	$aunmediated
	$bn
	$2rdamedia
338	$avolume
	$bnc
	$2rdacarrier

This change reflects RDA's determination to separate content and carrier information – one failing it identifies in AACR2 is its reliance on the format of items in order to determine the cataloguing rules that apply.

Some changes feel very AACR3. For example, the Old Testament and the New Testament are no longer abbreviated to 'O.T.' and 'N.T' but simply entered as:

```
130 0 $aBible. $pOld Testament
130 0 $aBible. $pNew Testament
```

This is something that most cataloguers have been looking forward to for years. Similarly, books of the Bible are no longer 'nested' inside the relevant testament:

```
130 0 $aBible. $pGenesis
```

Other changes are more fundamental, and reflect a change in ethos. For example, transcription was always a feature of AACR2, but in RDA it is safe to say that the text on the item is preferred over abbreviations and other devices for ensuring consistency in the appearance of catalogue records.

So, if a book says 'Second edition', under **RDA 1.2B** we enter 'Second edition' in the edition statement. We do *not* abbreviate it to '2nd ed.' as AACR2 required. Similarly, if a title contains a misspelling, we do not use '[sic]' to indicate the misspelling – we transcribe the title as it appears on the title page and simply add a variant title entry for the correct spelling.

In fact, we do not use Latin at all in RDA. As outlined in previous chapters, there is no more '[s.l.]' for unknown places in the publication area, nor '[s.n.]' for unknown publishers. Instead, we have '[Place of publication not identified]' and '[Publisher not identified]' – or the equivalent phrases in the language of the cataloguing agency.

Where the publisher is identified, **RDA 2.8.1.4** instructs us to transcribe it as it appears on the publication. We should not ignore words like 'Press', 'Co.' and 'Books' as we did under AACR2, where, apart from university presses, we were expected to give publisher names in their shortest internationally recognizable form.

Similarly, under **RDA 2.8.4.5**, where there is more than one publisher, we should list them all as they appear on the publication. This is in keeping with RDA's emphasis on relationships and discoverability.

As will be discussed in more detail below, relationships between publications, and between publications and their creators and owners, are at the core of RDA. Looking to *Functional Requirements for Bibliographic Records* and *Functional Requirements for Authority Data*, RDA highlights relationships as an aid to discoverability not only in the library environment, but beyond.

As part of this move, one rule change that provoked an outcry at the constituency review stage was the decision to do away with the rule of three. Under **RDA 2.4.1.5**, all people involved in the creation of a publication should be given an access point. An option has been created so that institutions can continue to employ the rule of three, but, as has been argued in earlier chapters, this still represents a shift from the rule of three as the usual practice to its being merely an option.

This section has only highlighted major changes in RDA. There are presentations on the JSC website that go into great detail about the changes (Joint Steering Committee for the Development of RDA, 2010b). Robert Maxwell's May 2010 presentation to the Utah Library Association is particularly accessible.

Here we should issue a caveat: the adoption of RDA is going to be much more akin to common law than statute law. Just as in common law countries, the elected politicians make the law, but the judges implement it, nuancing it and creating the law in practice, in the case of RDA, the JSC has created the new code, but the national libraries will be the places to whose policies we all look for practice guidelines.

The development of RDA and its principles

The Joint Steering Committee for the Development of RDA (formerly the JSC for AACR2) is always, rightfully, keen to point out that the new standard is rooted not only in AACR2, ISBD and the International Statement of Cataloguing Principles, but in the long line of history, from Panizzi's *Rules for the Compilation of the Catalogue* (British Museum Department of Printed Books, 1841) onwards.

In Chapter 1 we discussed Cutter's *Rules for a Dictionary Catalogue* and the influence that it has had on cataloguing ever since, foregrounding the centrality of the user in every cataloguing decision that we make, but his 'objects', 'means' and 'reasons for choice' are worth repeating here as they are so fundamental to the development of the new standard:

OBJECTS
4.   To enable a person to find a book of which either
     A. the author

B. the title

C. the subject is known

5.   To show what the library has

G. by a given author

H. on a given subject

I. in a given kind of literature

6.   To assist in the choice of a book

I. as to its edition (bibliographically)

J. as to its character (literary or topical)

MEANS

6.   Author-entry with the necessary references (for A and D).

7.   Title-entry or title-reference (for B).

8.   Subject-entry, cross-references, and classed subject-table (for C and E).

9.   Form-entry (for F).

10. Notes (for G and H).

REASONS FOR CHOICE

Other things being equal, choose the entry

(4)   That will probably be the first looked under by the class of people who use the library;

(5)   That is consistent with other entries, so that one principle can cover all;

(6)   That will mass entries least in places where it is difficult to so arrange them that they can be readily found, as under names of nations and cities.

(Cutter, 1891)

The commentator William Denton has described Cutter's Objects as 'the first set of axioms made in cataloging'. Denton's argument that there are four core ideas flowing through Anglo-American cataloguing is helpful, as it allows us to interrogate any cataloguing standard to see not only how it fits into cataloguing history, but also how fit for purpose it is. Denton's four core ideas are:

- the use of axioms to explain the purpose of catalogues
- the importance of user needs

- the idea of the 'work'
- standardization and internationalization (Denton, 2007).

Denton defines an axiom in practical terms as 'a core set of simple, fundamental principles that form the basis for complete cataloging codes such as *Anglo-American Cataloguing Rules*'. Unlike Panizzi's work, which consolidated organic growth at the British Museum and gave it some structure, Cutter's 'objects' start with basic principles which are then carried out by his 'means'.

However, Denton points out that Cutter's 'means' are not the only ways to satisfy his 'objects': 'It's possible for someone to start with Cutter's axioms and build up a different set of rules.' In essence, this is what we can see happening with the *Functional Requirements for Bibliographic Records*, which builds on Cutter's 'means' to form its user tasks:

> The functional requirements for bibliographic records are defined in relation to the following generic tasks that are performed by users when searching and making use of national bibliographies and library catalogues:
>
> - using the data to find materials that correspond to the user's stated search criteria (e.g. in the context of a search for all documents on a given subject, or a search for a recording issued under a particular title);
> - using the data retrieved to identify an entity (e.g. to confirm that the document described in a record corresponds to the document sought by the user, or to distinguish between two texts or recordings that have the same title);
> - using the data to select an entity that is appropriate to the user's needs (e.g. to select a text in a language the user understands, or to choose a version of a computer program that is compatible with the hardware and operating system available to the user);
> - using the data in order to acquire or obtain access to the entity described (e.g. to place a purchase order for a publication, to submit a request for the loan of a copy of a book in a library's collection, or to access online an electronic document stored on a remote computer).
>
> (IFLA Study Group on the Functional Requirements
> for Bibliographic Records, 2009)

The final user task, 'to acquire or obtain access', can be seen to have been implicit in Cutter's rules, since they were for a dictionary catalogue relating to the library's holdings. FRBR, written for the internet age, has to make this assumption explicit, since our cataloguing activities may include both our library's holdings and externally hosted material, accessed via the web.

If RDA is to be seen as the cataloguing code for the online era, FRBR should be seen as its foundation, containing the axioms on which RDA's rules are built. As Barbara Tillett has put it:

> FRBR describes the entities in the bibliographic universe, their relationships and attributes. It describes user tasks that serve as criteria to determine which attributes and relationships are important to include in a bibliographic description. FRBR also includes what were considered in the mid-1990s to be the mandatory data elements (attributes) to include in a national bibliographic record.
>
> All of these features of FRBR are incorporated into the new cataloging code... RDA: Resource Description and Access...
>
> RDA is intended to be a set of instructions for the content of descriptive metadata, whether packaged as a bibliographic record, an authority record, or some other structure.
>
> (Tillett, 2007)

FRBR as the foundation of RDA

As you read this you might be thinking that we have departed from practical cataloguing into the realms of cataloguing theory. Viewed from one perspective, you might be right. However, to understand RDA and its application, we need to understand the principles behind it, and, if nothing else (and as always in cataloguing), we need to learn the terminology.

Those who do not like RDA or FRBR often criticize the vocabulary that they use. One advantage of AACR2's structure consisting of chapters relating to particular formats is that the authors of the code could refer to something solid and tangible, and therefore easy for readers to visualize and understand. For example, in AACR2 Chapter 2 we read about monographs and printed books, while in AACR2 Chapter 6 we deal with sound recordings.

RDA is not structured according to format – in principle every rule can be applied to any format (unless a specific instruction is given within a rule exempting a particular format from it). This means that the authors have to use a more generic set of terms – which encompass everything from printed books through cartographic materials to websites. It even has to leave space for formats as yet unknown to us and still to be invented. The terms used in RDA are drawn directly from FRBR, and experience shows that cataloguers either love them or loathe them.

FRBR and RDA describe the units of bibliographic description as **entities**, and these entities are arranged in three groups:

> **Group 1 Entities: Work, Expression, Manifestation, and Item**
> **Group 2 Entities: Person, Corporate Body**
> **Group 3 Entities: Concept, Object, Event, Place.** (IFLA Study Group on the
> Functional Requirements for Bibliographic Records, 2009)

These entities can relate to each other in different ways, and some of our time as cataloguers will, under FRBR and RDA, be spent making these relationships explicit.

The observant reader will recall that Denton identified 'the idea of the "work"' as one of the four core ideas running through the history of Anglo-American cataloguing. Indeed, those of us trained under AACR2 or previous codes have become accustomed to using the term 'work' in a variety of ways, depending on the context in which we are speaking.

FRBR fixes its meaning as '**a distinct intellectual or artistic creation**' and offers this further explanation:

> A *work* is an abstract entity; there is no single material object one can point to as
> the *work*. We recognize the *work* through individual realizations or *expressions* of
> the *work*, but the *work* itself exists only in the commonality of content between
> and among the various *expressions* of the *work*. When we speak of Homer's *Iliad* as
> a *work*, our point of reference is not a particular recitation or text of the *work*, but
> the intellectual creation that lies behind all the various *expressions* of the *work*.
> (IFLA Study Group on the Functional Requirements for
> Bibliographic Records, 2009)

Those used to rare books cataloguing may recognize the endeavour to get as close to the idea of the text in the author's mind, while anyone who has read

Jasper Fforde's Thursday Next series of adventures may visualize a *work* as the master copy lodged in the Great Library and from which all other copies are derived (Fforde, 2002; 2003). One practical way to think of this abstract idea is to think of something that exists in different editions and languages – perhaps Mary Shelley's *Frankenstein* – and think of the *work* as the *essence* of the book that *remains* as *Frankenstein* even though it is *expressed* as a text and is *still Frankenstein* through each and every *imprint, edition* and *translation*.

FRBR tells us that 'A work is realized through an *expression*', and it defines an expression as 'the intellectual or artistic realization of a *work* in the form of alpha-numeric, musical, or choreographic notation, sound, image, object, movement, etc., or any combination of such forms' (IFLA Study Group on the Functional Requirements for Bibliographic Records, 2009).

One way to think of the *expression* is as the work expressed but not yet embodied. So if Dumas' *work* is the creation we know in English as *The Three Musketeers*, its first *expression* will have been its text in French, while the translation of the text into English is a later *expression* of the same work. Similarly, Beethoven's *Piano Sonata No. 14 in C# Minor (Moonlight Sonata)* is a work that has been *expressed* in the composer's notated music, and then as different *expressions* in each different notation used by performers over the years:

An expression is embodied in a *manifestation*.
> (IFLA Study Group on the Functional Requirements for
> Bibliographic Records, 2009)

If we think of Dumas, we can see that the original 1844 publication of *Les Trois Mousquetaires* is the *manifestation* of the first *expression* of the *work*, and the publication of each of the English translations are manifestations of further expressions. If we think of the *Moonlight Sonata*, we must think in terms of *recordings*: each separate recording of a particular notation is a *manifestation*.

FRBR specifies 'Changes that occur deliberately or even inadvertently in the production process that affect the copies result, strictly speaking, in a new *manifestation*. A *manifestation* resulting from such a change may be identified as a particular "state" or "issue" of the publication' (IFLA Study Group on the Functional Requirements for Bibliographic Records, 2009). This means that each new edition in the true sense of the word (a publication that incorporates new material) forms a new *manifestation*.

Finally in Group 1, '**A manifestation is exemplified by an** *item*'. This can be a difficult concept to grasp, because when we are dealing with mass-produced items like books, videos and CDs, the item and the manifestation can appear to be the same. Whereas manifestations are distinguished by changes that occur *during* production, items can be disambiguated from each other through changes *after* the production process ceases, such as damage or provenance markings.

Here is an example of a remarkable *item*, which exemplifies a fairly mundane *manifestation*. Minor (and today largely forgotten) poet Samuel Rogers (1763-1855) conceived of a *work* that was *expressed* as *Pleasures of Memory*, embodied in over 15 editions, or *manifestations*. One of these, published in 1810, has become a very well noted *item* following the addition of an original manuscript poem by Rogers' famous friend, Lord Byron (UCL, 2006).

Having the identifiable concept of the 'item' allows us to think and talk about adding copy-specific details, like provenance information – as you can be sure UCL's rare books librarian added to her catalogue record for this particular Rogers '*item*'.

If we go back to our original example, Shelley's *Frankenstein*, we can picture some of the Group 1 entities for the text as shown in Figure 5.1 on the next page.

Of course, each translation into a different language would result in a different *expression*, and since 1818 there have been many more *manifestations* of *Frankenstein*, and even more *items* for each *manifestation*.

Beware of this distinction in FRBR, though:

> When the modification of a *work* involves a significant degree of independent intellectual or artistic effort, the result is viewed, for the purpose of this study, as a new *work*. Thus paraphrases, rewritings, adaptations for children, parodies, musical variations on a theme and free transcriptions of a musical composition are considered to represent new *works*. Similarly, adaptations of a *work* from one literary or art form to another (e.g. dramatizations, adaptations from one medium of the graphic arts to another, etc.) are considered to represent new *works*. Abstracts, digests and summaries are also considered to represent new *works*.
>
> (IFLA Study Group on the Functional Requirements for
> Bibliographic Records, 2009)

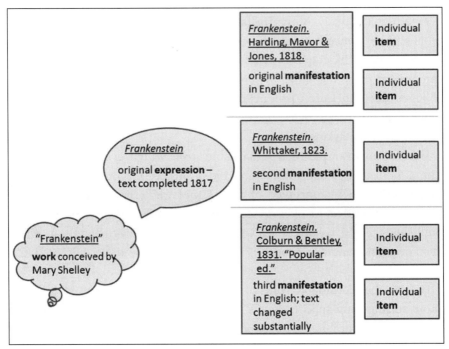

Figure 5.1 *Group 1 entities for Shelley's Frankenstein (Source: Welsh, 2009)*

This means that *film* adaptations of *Frankenstein* would begin as new, though related, works, with their own *expression(s)*, *manifestation(s)* and *item(s)*.

Relationships between entity groups

Group 2 entities are related to Group 1 entities through a degree of responsibility for their creation. To FRBR's *persons* and *corporate body*, RDA adds the concept of the *family* (as, for example, where a family is responsible for correspondence, like the Austen family letters). The idea of a relationship through responsibility for the creation of something is familiar to us from AACR2 and earlier models of cataloguing, but it is worth gaining familiarity with the ways in which FRBR (and later RDA) describe the generic **'responsibility relationships'**:

- A work is created by a person/corporate body [/family]
- An expression is realized by a person/corporate body [/family]

- A manifestation is produced by a person/corporate body [/family]
- An item is owned by a person/corporate body [/family].

(IFLA Study Group on the Functional Requirements for
Bibliographic Records, 2009)

Often in class, this statement of the relationship between an item and Group 2 entities helps students to grasp, once and for all, the difference between a manifestation and an item.

Group 3 entities describe a '**subject relationship**'. Although subject cataloguing *per se* is outwith the scope of this book, for the sake of completeness, it is worth pointing out that while a work can have as a subject any of the Group 3 entities – concept, object, event and/or place – FRBR also points out that it may also or instead have as a subject a Group 2 entity – person or corporate body [or family] – and/or it may also or instead have as a subject a Group 1 entity – work, expression, manifestation or item.

The explicit statement of relationships is a key feature of FRBR, and one of the features that readies it, and RDA based on it, to offer information outside our familiar library environment of the bibliographic record.

In the library we are used to interpreting fields of information within the context of the record as a whole. So when we see '**Fforde, Jasper**' as the main entry for a record (MARC field 100), we know that Jasper Fforde is the person of chief responsibility for the work described. In the title area, when we see 'Lost in a good book / Jasper Fforde' (MARC 245 10 $aLost in a good book / $cJasper Fforde), we know that what follows the ' / ' (MARC 245 $c) is the statement of responsibility. We also know that when there is no explicit description of the responsibility – 'by', 'compiled by', 'edited by', 'illustrated by' and so on – we should *infer* a creator responsibility, usually (for text) an authorial responsibility. We can only say that the responsibility is *usually* authorial, because in some cases the word 'author' does not make sense – a photographer would not think of herself as the *author* of a collection of her photographs, for example; nor would a cartographer think of herself as the *author* of one of her maps.

So we can see that in reading catalogue information, at least two significant judgements are being made, according to context:

- We are identifying the relationship between the people named and the work described using contextual information provided by the bibliographic record as a whole.
- We are nuancing the *kind* of relationship based on not only punctuation and coding within the record, but also a much wider context – our knowledge of the type of material described, and the *usual* way(s) in which creative or intellectual responsibility for that type of material is phrased.

When proponents of FRBR and RDA speak about their having relevance outside the library environment, they describe applications within the semantic web – the next generation of the internet, in which computers are able to contextualize and nuance information, or, in the shorter term, in which we humans present information in such a way that computers have enough details to contextualize and nuance it. They also advocate a linked data approach – that instead of the smallest unit of useful bibliographic information being the record, it should be possible to link data field by field.

If we stay with Group 2 entities we can see an option to provide more specific information about the relationship of *some* people to *some* texts has been provided through AACR2 and MARC.

AACR2 21.0D provides an *'optional addition'* for '**Designations of function**':

21.0D1. In the cases noted below, add an abbreviated designation of the function to an added entry heading for a person.

FUNCTION PERFORMED	DESIGNATION
compiler	*comp.*
editor	*ed.*
illustrator	*ill.*
translator	*tr.*

Add other designations to headings as instructed in particular rules.
In specialist or archival cataloguing, when desirable for identification or file arrangement, add designations from standard lists appropriate to the material being catalogued.

In the card catalogue environment, this allows for cards in which the named person is the author (main entry) to file ahead of the cards in which the named person is, say, the illustrator (normally added entry). For example, Eric Gill's treatise *An essay on typography* would have the main entry '**Gill, Eric**' while his equally famous illustration work on *The Canterbury Tales* (Golden Cockerell, 1929-31) would have a main entry card filed under '**Chaucer, Geoffrey**' and an added entry card filed under '**Gill, Eric,** *ill.*'. In the catalogue drawer, there would be a small run of cards headed '**Gill, Eric**' followed by a long run of cards for '**Gill, Eric,** *ill.*'. We can see that some library users would be interested in Gill as a writer, some would be interested in him as an illustrator or artist, and some would be interested in all of his work.

We can also see that a happy byproduct of the heading '**Gill, Eric,** *ill.*' is that we do not need to rely on the title area statement of responsibility in order to work out Eric Gill's role in *The Canterbury Tales* (Golden Cockerell, 1929-31). In FRBR-speak, the Group 1 entity *The Canterbury Tales* is illustrated by the Group 2 entity Eric Gill.

Similarly, in MARC 21 Authority Data, the 100 $e **relator term** allows for the 'Designation of function that describes the relationship between a name and a work', as in this example (in which $t is the title of the work, and $l its language):

100 1#$aBlum, Leon,$d1872-1950,$edefendant$tLeon Blum devant la Cour supreme, Riom.$lHebrew

There are several other places in AACR2 and MARC where we can see opportunities for linked data – name title references provide information about relationships between Group 1 and Group 2 entities, while we can see relationships between Group 1 entities and other Group 1 entities through such features are alternative titles and series tracings.

However, the usual iterations of AACR2 and MARC 21 in most library settings have limited linked data possibilities. Many do not use the uniform title option to collocated diversely titled examples of works. Most do not use the option provided at **AACR2 21.0D1** or MARC Authority format 100 $e.

In essence, our online library catalogues are structured as large relational databases in which the relationships expressed occur at the level of the complete bibliographic record.

Some metasearch engines employ sophisticated parsing algorithms in order to display our catalogues as linked data, but the algorithms required are complex, and therefore costly and, at the current state of the art, not 100% accurate.

Advocates of FRBR and RDA promote them as opportunities to rethink and, more significantly, redisplay the library catalogue record in such a way that its data could be served up in smaller portions to applications outside the library's walls.

However, one problem with the take-up of FRBR at a practical level, which may similarly inhibit the adoption of RDA, is the difficulty of seeing records in action. At the CILIP Executive Briefing on RDA on 12 April 2011 we were somewhat startled in the final session when one delegate asked 'Can you show me an RDA record in an RDA environment?'

At the moment, the answer to this is 'No''. We can see quite a few RDA records in the MARC environment, but the IT systems are not yet in place to see RDA in a linked data environment.

One of the aims of the US national tests of RDA was to ensure that all records created as RDA were compatible with existing systems. On a practical level this makes a lot of sense, because in the current financial climate we cannot imagine any libraries having the resources to convert their entire legacy data from AACR2 in MARC to RDA, and so, for the US tests, the data created can best be described as RDA in MARC. For example, here is the first record from the Library of Congress test data file:

```
=LDR 01570nam a2200373Ki 4500
=001 ocn697793103
=003 OCoLC
=005 20110201055509.0
=008 110121s2011\\\\at\\\\\\\\\\\\001\0\eng\d
=010 \\$a 2009941964
=040 \\$aOCLCQ$beng$erda$cQBX
=020 \\$a9780538754286 (Student edition)
=020 \\$a0538754281 (Student edition)
=020 \\$z9780538754293 (Instructor's edition)
=020 \\$z053875429X (Instructor's edition)
=035 \\$a(OCoLC)697793103
```

=037 \ \$aONLY US RDA TEST PARTICIPANTS SHOULD ADD INSTITUTION
RECORDS TO THIS MASTER RECORD; NO CHANGES SHOULD BE MADE
TO THE MASTER RECORD
=079 \ \$aocn664722928
=049 \ \$aQBXA
=100 1\$aGwartney, James D.
=245 10$aMacroeconomics:$bprivate and public choice /$cJames D.
Gwartney, Richard L. Stroup, Russell S. Sobel, David A. Macpherson.
=250 \ \$a13th edition, 13e, Student edition.
=260
\ \$aAustralia;$aBrazil;$aJapan;$aKorea;$aMexico;$aSingapore;$aSpain;$aUnite
d Kingdom;$aUnited States:$bSouth-Western Cengage Learning,$c[2011],
copyright 2011.
=300 \ \$axxvii, 585 pages;$c28 cm
=336 \ \$atext$2rdacontent
=337 \ \$aunmediated$2rdamedia
=338 \ \$avolume$2rdacarrier
=500 \ \$aIncludes index.
=505 0\$aThe economic way of thinking — Markets and government — Core
macroeconomics — International economics — Applying the basics: special
topics in economics.
=700 1\$aStroup, Richard L.
=700 1\$aSobel, Russell S.
=700 1\$aMacpherson, David A.
=985 \ \$acommonsetA$bIOrQBI
=994 \ \$aC0$bDLC

(Library of Congress Cataloging and Acquisitions, 2011)

If we look at only the fields in which we would hope to see a relationship
between Group 1 and Group 2 entities expressed explicitly, we have:

=100 1\$aGwartney, James D.
=245 10$aMacroeconomics:$bprivate and public choice /$cJames D.
Gwartney, Richard L. Stroup, Russell S. Sobel, David A. Macpherson.
=250 \\$a13th edition, 13e, Student edition.
=700 1\$aStroup, Richard L.

```
=700 1\$aSobel, Russell S.
=700 1\$aMacpherson, David A.
```

As far as Group 1 is concerned, we can see that we have the description of an **item** which is a **manifestation** (13th edition) of an **expression** of the **work** *Macroeconomics: private and public choice.*

We can see four Group 2 entities – James D. Gwartney, Richard L. Stroup, Russell S. Sobel and David A. Macpherson.

Under RDA, we would hope to see the relationship between these Group 1 and Group 2 entities made explicit, but here it is still implicit. From the statement of responsibility '/ James D. Gwartney, Richard L. Stroup, Russell S. Sobel, David A. Macpherson' we are left, as in AACR2, to *infer* that these four people are co-authors. There is no relator code in the 100 and 700 $e to make it explicit that they are *co-authors*. We are inferring that this is text material, and that authorship is the correct phrase for creation.

We can also see that despite RDA's stance that the concept of main entry and added entry should no longer be put into practice, here, in the MARC code, we have the first-named author, Gwartney, given the 100, *main* entry, while the others are 700, *added* entries.

The rule of three has not been practised (under AACR2, we would have seen only Gwartney in the statement of responsibility, and he would have been entered as a 700 added entry while the title was promoted to main entry(245 first indicator 0). In RDA, the rule of three is an option, with the provision of entries for all co-authors the usual practice.

Finally, from this entry, it is not possible to tell whether these co-authors have been responsible for only this edition of *Macroeconomics: private and public choice* or if they have all been responsible for all 13 editions. We are left to infer their role from the positioning of the statement of responsibility in the title area and not the edition area. We assume that they have been responsible from the first edition onwards.

This is not linked data. But then, nor is it what the questioner wanted on 12 April – an RDA record in an RDA environment. It is RDA, a code designed for a linked data environment, rendered in MARC, a data exchange format designed for a flatter, relational database structure.

FRBRizing the catalogue

RDA is brand new, so it is perhaps not surprising that examples have not yet been created for an RDA systems environment. So again, we look back to FRBR.

Since FRBR's first publication in 1997, many articles have been written about 'FRBRizing the catalog', but examples of catalogues constructed along fully FRBRized lines are still hard to find. At the CILIP Executive Briefing on RDA on 12 April 2011 Alan Danskin referred to Indiana University's *Variations/FRBR: variations as a testbed for the FRBR Conceptual Model* (www.dlib.indiana.edu/projects/vfrbr/index.shtml). This research project, which runs until September 2011, provides a search interface based on FRBR principles and includes records mapped from MARC to FRBR, and includes documentation on how Group 2 entities and Group 1 entities relationship structures were created (Indiana University Variations/FRBR Project, 2010).

In the search interface, a simple search for 'Moonlight sonata' retrieves a list divided into 'works' (of which there is one, '*Sonatas*, **piano, no. 14, op. 27, no. 2, C# minor Beethoven, Ludwig van (1770-1827)**') and 'Recordings/scores' (of which there are over 50, all of them relevant to the search). The full record for the **work** includes variant titles, 'composer variants' (Beethoven's name expressed in different forms and scripts), key, instruments and subject headings. Each of the records for recordings or scores links through to the university's standard online catalogue record.

In contrast, a basic keyword search for 'Moonlight sonata' on Indiana University's standard online library catalogue returns over 100 results, displayed in reverse chronological order.

Comparing the two ways to access the catalogue records, we can see that *Variations/FRBR* presents users with a hierarchical results list, in which the first record(s) displayed in the section headed 'Works' provides contextual information, and that each of the records in the 'Recordings/scores' section has a clear, explicit relationship to the work of which it is an expression or manifestation.

We might observe that this type of search has a closer affinity in 'look and feel' to the type of searching with which we are familiar on the web, and which is facilitated by a range of metadata standards.

This, then, is the aspiration for RDA: it should continue to support traditional library catalogues, in which it should be compatible with records created under AACR2 and previous cataloguing codes, but that it should present opportunities for future developments, outside and inside the library. As Chris Oliver has put it: 'There are advantages that will be seen on day one, advantages that will require a sufficiently large body of RDA data before they become apparent, advantages that necessitate software improvements to fully exploit the changes, and, finally, advantages that will be realized in future Web environments' (2010).

A colleague in library record supply often observes that in creating bibliographic records that can be useful to libraries with different levels of requirements, she feels that record agencies 'build a Rolls-Royce, for most libraries to buy only the bits that could make up a tricycle'. Perhaps the immediate future, for libraries that adopt RDA, will feel a little like that: perhaps we will be creating records for a semantic web that has not yet arrived, and for a library OPAC (Online Public Access Catalogue) offering that is a few years in the future.

What is clear is that *now* is not the time to move to RDA. However, there are libraries that have already made the transition to RDA. The universities of Stanford and Chicago, which both participated in the US tests, are continuing to catalogue in RDA.

Director of Metadata and Cataloging Services at the University of Chicago, Christopher Cronin has stated publicly in presentations about RDA that in order to take part in the tests he and his team had to commit to moving completely to the new standard. Typically of most universities, the cataloguing team is fairly small, and it would not have been cost or time efficient for them to have catalogued according to AACR2 *and* RDA (as larger libraries like the Library of Congress did for their RDA test data). Similarly, the cost of training everyone to catalogue in RDA and making the few systems changes required for RDA in MARC can only, really, be justified by a real move to the standard.

For libraries taking part in and downloading records from consortia such as OCLC, this means that RDA has, to some extent, already arrived. Celine Carty (University of Cambridge) and other cataloguing team leaders have already started to find records coded MARC 040 $e rda appearing in records downloaded by their acquisitions team and paraprofessional staff.

As Celine points out, because some RDA is so new, some of these records really are 'full' RDA, while others are only partially so, therefore staff working with these records have to work out what to do with them.

One message from the CILIP Executive Briefing on 12 April 2011, and from previous meetings and training events in the USA, is that adoption of RDA is unlikely to be 'wholesale'. Because there are so many options in the new standard each library, or at least each consortia, may well create its own RDA profile, consisting of its own choices of options. Many will follow the decisions of the Library of Congress, and in the UK the British Library, but in the meantime, the hybrid record is already here.

Practical cataloguing today

What does this mean for practical cataloguing? For those in libraries small enough to be creating most of their own records, the best advice is to do nothing yet, but be aware when you are looking at other people's online catalogues as reference sources for thorny issues that you may start to see features that are from RDA rather than AACR2.

For those in libraries that contribute to consortia, 'it is probably best to follow discussion documents issued and attend trainings organized by your consortium. For example, on 5 April 2011 the Program for Cooperative Cataloging Policy Committee issued *PoCo Discussion Paper on RDA Implementation Alternatives*. It is actively seeking discussion among members of the PCC, and is also a useful indication of the kinds of issues that will be faced by all consortia.

For those in libraries of all sizes, the best actions in 2012 are to wait and see, but to continue to prepare staff for change. Preparation activities include:

- familiarizing oneself with the language of RDA, and its underlying concepts, which, as outlined here, are both rooted in FRBR
- keeping up to date with announcements from the US tests at www.loc.gov/catdir/cpso/RDAtest/rdatest.html
- perhaps using some of the training tools at www.loc.gov/catdir/cpso/RDAtest/rdatest.html which include webcasts as well as text-based resources
- looking out for RDA records creeping into any databases that you use, and taking time to familiarize yourself with them.

Depending on your management situation, it might also be worth updating your in-house data on how long your current workflow takes, using AACR2. Any change involves some initial drop in productivity while staff become familiar with new ways of working, and it is always useful to have records of how long existing procedures take, to act as a benchmark throughout future change processes.

6

AACR and RDA

Introduction

Unsurprisingly, one of the frequently asked questions on the RDA website is 'Will I have to make changes to my cataloguing records?' The official answer given is:

> The JSC agreed early on that records created by using RDA would be compatible with AACR2 records and that any instance where incompatibility might exist would be scrutinized very carefully before recommending a change. This commitment holds true today. But, there will be a few instances where headings will require modification, such as the headings for 'Bible'. Using computers' abilities for global updating will make these changes considerably easier than in pre-online system days.
>
> (Joint Steering Committee for the Development of RDA, 2010a)

This chapter takes as its starting point an example record from Appendix M in the draft of RDA (Joint Steering Committee for the Development of RDA, 2008a and b) and compares it with a record produced under AACR2.

We are working from the text published on 31 October 2008, which the Joint Steering Committee issued as a draft and acknowledged contained typographic and other errors. We have corrected these in the light of the examples issued by the Library of Congress in 2011 (Library of Congress Cataloging and Acquisitions, 2011).

Example: Book 1
Taylor, Arlene G. *The organization of information*. **2nd ed. London: Libraries Unlimited, 2004**.

Table 6.1 on the following pages maps the information in Appendix M to the existing record on the Library of Congress website (Library of Congress, 2003). The information is listed in the order set by the RDA elements section of Appendix M. A blank space in the table means we could not find an equivalent.

Let us work through the equivalency table and discuss how it exemplifies the similarities and differences between RDA and AACR2.

Title proper

RDA 2.2.2 deals with the 'preferred source of information' – the new term for AACR2's 'chief source of information'. **RDA 2.2.2.2** specifies the preferred source for 'Resources consisting of one or more pages, leaves, sheets or cards (or images of one or more pages, leaves sheets or cards)'. As a standard book, our title meets these criteria. There is no change here from AACR2 – we are instructed to 'use the title page, title sheet, or title card (or image thereof) as the preferred source of information'.

RDA 2.3.1.4 'Recording titles' instructs us to 'Transcribe a title as it appears on the source of information. Apply the general guidelines on transcription given under **1.7**', which deals with abbreviations, punctuation and diacriticals.

Already we can see that RDA requires us to move swiftly between different rules. This applies the same principle we are used to in AACR2, where rules are not restated, but referenced.

If the amount of cross references seems greater in RDA, the explanation is that the new code has been designed as an online product, and the RDA toolkit promises to take full advantage of hypertext linking. Relevant rules appear collocated in the appropriate parts of the toolkit, so that if we are looking at **2.3.1.4**, we are automatically served with **1.7** as well. So we should not think of ourselves flicking between pages in a looseleaf (like AACR2) but of the computer creating the correct display for us on the fly – a concept familiar to us in standard modern OPACs where holdings records and bibliographic records are amalgamated on the fly to create the appropriate display.

But, to return to the Title proper, we can see that there is essentially no difference between AACR2 and RDA. The title proper is taken from the title page of the book, in exactly the way that AACR2 specified we create the title statement.

Table 6.1

			From RDA Draft. Appendix M (with minor amendments)				From lccn.loc.gov/2003058904		
RDA Ref	RDA Element	Data Recorded	MARC Field Tag	MARC Field	Indicators	Data Recorded	MARC Field Tag	Indicators	Data Recorded
			Leader/06	Type of record		a	000/06		a
			Leader/07	Bibliographic level		m	000/07		m
			007/00	Physical description fixed field - Category of material		t	007		t
			008/35-37	Fixed-length data elements - Language		eng	008		eng
2.3.2	Title proper	The organization of information	245	Title statement	14	$a The organization of information /	245	14	$a The organization of information /
2.4.2	Statement of responsibility relating to title	Arlene G. Taylor	245	Title statement	14	$c Arlene G. Taylor.	245	14	$c Arlene G. Taylor.
2.5.2	Designation of edition	Second edition	250	Edition statement	##	$a Second edition.	250	##	$a 2nd ed.
2.8.2	Place of publication	Westport, Connecticut	260	Publication, distribution, etc. (Imprint)	##	$a Westport, Connecticut ;	260	##	$a Westport, Conn. :

(continued)

Table 6.1 (*continued*)

		From RDA Draft. Appendix M (with minor amendments)					From lccn.loc.gov/2003058904		
RDA Ref	RDA Element	Data Recorded	MARC Field Tag	MARC Field	Indicators	Data Recorded	MARC Field Tag	Indicators	Data Recorded
2.8.2	Place of publication	London	260	Publication, distribution, etc. (Imprint)	##	$a London :			
2.8.4	Publisher's name	Libraries Unlimited, a member of the Greenwood Publishing Group	260	Publication, distribution, etc. (Imprint)	##	$b Libraries Unlimited, a member of the Greenwood Publishing Group,	260	##	$b Libraries Unlimited,
2.11	Copyright date	©2004	260	Publication, distribution, etc. (Imprint)	##	$c ©2004.	260	##	$c 2004.
2.12.2	Title proper of series	Library and information science text series	490	Series statement	1#	$a Library and information science text series	440	#0	$a Library and information science text series
2.13	Mode of issuance	single unit							
2.15	Identifier for the manifestation	ISBN 1-56308-976-9	020	International Standard Book Number	##	$a 1563089769	020	##	$a 1563089769 (alk. paper)
2.15	Identifier for the manifestation	ISBN 1-56308-969-6 (paperback)	020					020	##	$a 1563089696 (pbk. : alk. paper)
3.2	Media type	unmediated							

(continued)

Table 6.1 (*continued*)

	From RDA Draft. Appendix M (with minor amendments)						From lccn.loc.gov/2003058904		
RDA Ref	RDA Element	Data Recorded	MARC Field Tag	MARC Field	Indicators	Data Recorded	MARC Field Tag	Indicators	Data Recorded
3.3	Carrier type	volume							
3.4	Extent of text	xxvii, 417 pages	300	Physical description	##	$a xxvii, 417 pages ;	300	##	$a xxvii, 417 p. ;
							300	##	$b ill. ;
3.5	Dimensions	27 cm	300	Physical description	##	$c 27 cm.	300	##	$c 27 cm.
4.3	Contact information	http://www.lu.com	037	Source of acquisition	##	http://www.lu.com			
6.10	Content type	text							
7.12	Language of the content	In English	546	Language note	##	In English.			
7.16	Supplementary content	Includes bibliography and index	504	Bibliography, etc. Note	##	Includes bibliography and index.	504	##	$a Includes bibliographical references (p. 385-405) and index.
19.2	Creator	Taylor, Arlene G., 1941-	100	Main entry - Personal name	1#	$a Taylor, Arlene G., 1941-	100	1#	$a Taylor, Arlene G., $d 1941-
25.1	Related work	Library and information science text series	830	Series added entry - Uniform title	#0	$a Library and information science text series	440	#0	$a Library and information science text series

If we look at the suggested MARC entry from RDA Appendix M, we can see that it is identical to the existing 245 entry for the record on the Library of Congress catalogue.

Statement of responsibility relating to title

RDA 2.4.1.1 defines a statement of responsibility as 'a statement relating to the identification and/or function of any persons, families, or corporate bodies responsible for the creation of, or contributing to the realization of, the intellectual or artistic content of a resource'. In the context of this example, Arlene G. Taylor is the author of the book, and so has a clear responsibility for its creation.

As in AACR2, **RDA 2.4.1.2** instructs us we should 'Take statements of responsibility from the same source as the associated title, designation of edition, designation of a named revision of an edition, title of a series, or title of a subseries'. Further, **2.4.2.2** instructs: 'Take statements of responsibility relating to title from the following sources (in order of preference):

a) the same source as the title proper (see **2.3.2.2**)
b) another source within the resource itself (see **2.2.2**)
c) one of the other sources of information specified under **2.2.4**.'

In our example, this is straightforward – Arlene G. Taylor is named as the author on the title page.

RDA 2.4.1.4 deals with recording statements of responsibility: 'Transcribe a statement of responsibility in the form in which it appears on the source of information.' Here we have only one short statement of responsibility, identifying the author. In fact, as an example, it is highly uncontentious.

However, if you're used to AACR2 conventions, it is worth noting that **RDA 2.4.1.4** includes the option to abridge a statement of responsibility 'only if it can be abridged without loss of essential information', and *without* using the marks of omission '...'.

RDA 2.4.1.5 is one of the most controversial changes proposed by the new standard. Dealing with 'Statement[s] naming more than one person, etc.' it instructs us to 'Record a statement of responsibility naming more than one person, etc., as a single statement regardless of whether the persons, families, or corporate bodies named in it perform the same function or different functions'. This effectively does away with one of the cataloguing decisions with which beginning cataloguers under AACR2 can struggle – deciding whether a responsibility is shared or mixed. Under RDA, this distinction does not matter: we simply record all contributors as they appear on the source of information in one statement of responsibility.

Few might object to a change that makes comprehension easier for those new to the discipline. The controversy in **RDA 2.4.1.5** is in its 'optional omission': 'If a single statement of responsibility names more than three persons, families, or corporate bodies performing the same function, or with the same degree of responsibility, omit all but the first of each group of such persons, families, or bodies.'

There has been debate on the cataloguing e-mail lists about the 'demise of the rule of three', and this rule within RDA implies that standard cataloguing will be to record *all* those with a responsibility, with there being an *option* to continue with the rule of three. Even if we choose to take that option, we should not continue to use AACR2's '... [et al.]' but should 'Indicate the omission by summarizing what has been omitted... Enclose the summary of the omission in square brackets'. The first example RDA gives us is:

Roger Colbourne [and six others]
Source of information reads: Roger Colbourne, Suzanne Bassett, Tony Billing, Helen McCormick, John McLennan, Andrew Nelson and Hugh Robertson

It will be obvious to anyone with experience in global editing on library management systems that implementing this change retrospectively across existing catalogue records requires a real human being to look at each item, decide what phrase should be entered to replace the existing marks of omission, and then enter that phrase in the record.

As with all the options included in RDA, those responsible for cataloguing policy will have to make a decision on how to deal with such cases. In 2012, we can look to consortia such as OCLC and COPAC, library management system designers and the MARC 21 standard for Bibliographic Data to provide us with public examples of best practice. Now that the US tests have reported, it is likely that statements from consortia will follow.

Designation of edition

Designation of edition is identified as a core element, although we are not instructed to enter information unless there is some sort of edition statement on the item we are cataloguing.

RDA 2.5.2 provides a useful scope note on the designation of edition, including a useful checklist of indications of designation of edition:

> In case of doubt about whether a statement is a designation of edition, consider the presence of a word such as edition, issue, release, level, state, or update (or its equivalent in another language), or a statement indicating:
>
> a) a difference in content
> b) a difference in geographic coverage
> c) a difference in language
> d) a difference in audience
> e) a particular format or physical presentation
> f) a different date associated with the content
>
> as evidence that such a statement is a designation of edition.

It is important to note that whereas under AACR2 we standardized the format of the entries in the edition statement, in RDA we enter the edition statement as it appears on the source.

In our example, we can see that the Library of Congress has followed **AACR2 1.2B1**, which instructs us to 'Use abbreviations as instructed in appendix B' and exemplifies '2nd ed. (*Source of information reads:* Second edition)'.

RDA Appendix M, faced with exactly this situation, renders the designation of edition as 'Second edition'.

Practice note

There are benefits for searching in entering the edition in a standardized form. If library users are likely to want to refine their search or sort their results by edition (for example when collating the many versions of a Shakespeare play), it may be better to continue using AACR2 practice and standardize the entry format.

In the example with which we are working there is no statement of responsibility relating to edition, but it is worth noting that instructions for dealing with this are given at **RDA 2.5.4.** Essentially, RDA treats statements of responsibility here in the same way as AACR2, and we should remember that in cases of doubt we should assume the statement of responsibility relates to title.

Place of publication

The rules set out at **RDA 2.8.2** dealing with place of publication have attracted debate in the cataloguing community. Before we get too deeply involved in the detail of this, we should note the statement: 'Publisher's name and date of publication are core elements for published resources. Place of publication is optional.' So, it is entirely possible for a cataloguing agency to opt out of using this field altogether while still being RDA-compliant.

The changes from AACR2 can be summarized as:

1 Record the place of publication including the 'name of larger jurisdiction... if present on the publication' (**RDA 2.8.2.3**). Examples given include:
   - Westport, Connecticut
   - Burlington, VT, USA
   - Aldershot, Hampshire, England
   - Tolworth, England
   - Lugduni Batavorum.
2 In cases with more than one place of publication, record *all* the places of publication 'in the order indicated by the sequence, layout, or typography of the names on the source of information' (**RDA 2.8.2.4**).
3 If we do not know and cannot identify or assume a place of publication, we should 'record *Place of publication not identified*'.

The first two of these changes have impacted on the example we have in hand. Under AACR2, the Library of Congress has abbreviated 'Westport, Connecticut' to 'Westport, Conn.' and has given only the first place of publication, omitting the second, UK, place of publication, London.

Many cataloguing agencies interpreted **AACR2 1.4C5** to give only the first named place of publication and, if they wish to adopt RDA fully, they will find their cataloguers taking a little longer over publications with more than one place of publication. Those who have catalogued in a law library might think of the many European Union publications that have a place of publication in each EU country (and currently we are up to 27 EU member states and growing).

A bigger impact will be on the consistency of the catalogue – clearly, to be consistent, we really should go back through existing catalogue entries and input all the places of publication. Since we are looking at blank fields, we can't make this change using a computerized global edit – a human being will have to identify which publications require entries in this field and then make them manually.

Fortunately, if we want to change all the former entries for 'Westport, Conn.' most library management systems can use a global edit facility to find all entries containing 'Conn.' in the place of publication field (MARC 260) and change it to 'Connecticut'.

Similarly, the change from **AACR2 1.4C6** in which we used '[s.l.]' to indicate 'sine loco' to **RDA 2.8.2.6** can be carried out using a global edit – as long as we have been consistent in our use of '[s.l.]' this will be a quick and painless process.

However, this throws up the question, if we can make only *some* of the changes required for the place of publication field to comply with RDA, should we do so, or are we confusing the user if we change some things but not *all* things? As was asked recently on a cataloguing e-mail discussion list, what percentage of our records need to follow RDA for us to say that our catalogue is RDA-compliant? (We have no answer from the JSC yet).

Again, this is something for which we look to the national libraries' trial and to the large cataloguing consortia to provide practical advice. However, as an academic, I can't help wondering if we are about to witness the application of a parallel world theory, where each policy decision we make leads to the further fragmentation of the standardization of the catalogue, which has been the main marker of the computer cataloguing era until now.

Publisher's name

In looking at our example, we can see that the current MARC record observes the instruction at **AACR2 1.4D2** to give the publisher's name in the shortest internationally recognizable form, 'Libraries Unlimited', while the suggested RDA entry is the more fulsome 'Libraries Unlimited, a member of the Greenwood Publishing Group'.

This reflects **RDA 2.8.1.4**, which instructs us to 'Transcribe places of publication and publishers' names in the form in which they appear on the source of information'. The same rule gives us an optional omission: 'Omit levels in a corporate hierarchy that are not required to identify the publisher. Do not use a mark of omission (...) to indicate such an omission.' Clearly, in compiling this example, the JSC has not taken this option.

The change is a subtle one – clearly we can take the option to give the publisher in its shortest possible form, but this is an *option*, and therefore, we might infer, weighted towards giving the hierarchy where it appears on the source of information (in this case, the title page).

A different kind of option is given to us with regard to books with more than one publisher. **RDA 2.8.4** opens with the 'core element' identifier, which states '*If more than one publisher's name appears on the source of information, only the first recorded is required*'. Then at **RDA 2.8.4.5**, which deals specifically with 'More than one publisher', we are instructed: 'If more than one person, family, or corporate body is named as a publisher of the resource, record the publishers' names in the order indicated by the sequence, layout, or typography of the names on the source of information.' In other words, we don't have to record all the publishers named, but we can if we want to do so.

This simplifies **AACR2 1.4D4**, which sets out the situations in which we should give more than one publisher's name, expanding on its original direction to 'describe it [the item] in terms of the first named [publisher] and the corresponding place(s)'.

Practice note

Many cataloguing agencies disregard the occasions set out at AACR2 1.4D4 and either opt to record all publishers all the time, or only the first named publisher, or the first-named publisher in the country of the cataloguing agency. It will be interesting to note how many agencies adopt RDA's option of simply recording the first-named publisher.

RDA 2.8.4.7 deals with instances in which we cannot identify the publisher. Whereas in **AACR2 1.46D** this was [s.n.] 'sine nomine or its equivalent in a nonroman script', now we are instructed to 'record *publisher not identified*'.

If we have been consistent in our use of '[s.n.]' we can simply employ a global edit to change existing records to the required new form, so although this is a change, it does not require a lot of manual effort.

Copyright date

RDA 2.8.6 states that the 'Date of publication' is a core element. **RDA 2.8.6.6** instructs: 'If the date of publication is not identified in a resource that is in a published form, record (in order of preference) the date of distribution (see **2.9.6**), the copyright date (see 2.11) or the date of manufacture (see **2.10.6**).' Only if all these dates are unidentifiable should we 'supply the date or approximate date of publication'.

The example is a little confusing, since the Library of Congress has stated the date of publication as being '2004' whereas the RDA example gives the copyright date. Although we agree with the Library of Congress that a publication date is present on the item, the use of the copyright date in the example does, at least, allow us to discuss it.

RDA 2.11 states: '*Copyright date is a core element if neither the date of publication nor the date of distribution is identified*'. The scope note at **RDA 2.11.1.1** informs us: 'A **copyright date** is a date associated with a claim of protection under copyright or a similar regime.' The rationale behind its importance is indicated in the further explanation that 'Copyright dates include phonogram dates (i.e., dates associated with claims of protection for sound recordings)'. It is obvious in the post-Napster era of intellectual property that the copyright date of an item is of growing importance. In any case, in music cataloguing, copyright date has always been important, and under RDA we should continue to record the most recent copyright date in this field.

While few might debate the importance of providing a copyright date, especially where no publication date is offered, controversy has surrounded the instruction at **RDA 2.11.1.3** to 'Precede the date by the copyright symbol (©) or the phonogram symbol (℗), or by *copyright* or *phonogram* if the appropriate symbol cannot be reproduced'. As a student using one of the major cataloguing systems remarked in a recent tutorial, 'Most library management systems can barely cope with rendering 'é' searchable as well as displayable, so how are they going to cope with symbols like that?' While we might query the harshness (and perhaps the syntax) of her comment, she is not alone in questioning the wisdom of encouraging the use of symbols as standard in catalogue records.

In that class the student group was split, as we feel the cataloguing community is split, by the question of the utility or otherwise of using 'c' for copyright as instructed by **AACR2 1.4F5** – 'c1949'. Half the group felt that users most commonly thought 'c' was an abbreviation for 'circa', whereas we cataloguers know that if we meant circa we would type 'ca. 1949' as directed by **AACR2 1.4F7**.

Practice note

Take care whenever you decide to introduce symbols and/or diacriticals into your cataloguing practice. It is of supreme importance that you test your library management system's ability to search, display and sort according to these marks before you use them. Remember that RDA 1.7.1 gives us the alternative: 'If the agency creating the data has established in-house guidelines for capitalization, punctuation, numerals, symbols, abbreviations, etc., or has designated a published style manual, etc., (e.g. *The Chicago Manual of Style*) as its preferred guide, use those guidelines or that style manual in place of the instructions given under RDA 1.7.2–1.7.9 below and in the appendices.'

Title proper of series

Title proper of series is identified as a core element, although we are not expected to enter anything here unless there is a statement on the item – many of the things we catalogue are not part of a series at all.

RDA 2.12.2 sets out how we should deal with items belonging to series. As we can see in our example, there is no real change from AACR2, including how we deal with statements of responsibility (**RDA 2.12.6**).

Mode of issuance

As set out in **RDA 2.13**, '**Mode of issuance** is a categorization reflecting whether a resource is issued in one or more parts, the way it is updated, and its intended termination.' **RDA 2.13.1.2** tells us that we can take information from any source if we cannot find what we need on the item itself.

There are four options:

- *Single unit* – self-explanatory and the most common in most collections. RDA gives us the examples of a single-volume monograph or a pdf.
- *Multipart monograph* – 'A resource issued in two or more parts (either simultaneously or successively) that is complete or intended to be completed within a finite number of parts (e.g. a dictionary in two volumes or three audiocassettes issued as a set).'
- *Serial* – RDA carries forward the standard definition of a serial as 'A resource issued in successive parts, usually bearing numbering, that has no predetermined conclusion (e.g. a periodical, a monographic series, or a newspaper)'. RDA further specifies that this mode if issuance 'Includes resources that exhibit characteristics of serials, such as successive issues, numbering, and frequency, but whose duration is limited (e.g. newsletters of events) and reproductions of serials'.
- *Integrating resource* – again, this is self-explanatory: a publication with updates that 'are integrated into the whole'. RDA suggests the examples of a looseleaf or a website.

Mode of issuance is not a core element, and it will be interesting to find out how many cataloguing agencies decide to use it.

Identifier for the manifestation

This is identified as a core element, although older items, such as books published before the introduction of ISBNs, do not have such an identifier, which **RDA 2.15** defines as an 'alphanumeric string associated with a manifestation that serves to differentiate that manifestation from other manifestations'.

Essentially this maps neatly to MARC 21 fields 020 and 022, so although we may be thrown at first by the vocabulary, recording this information is something that most cataloguing agencies have been doing as standard for a very long time indeed.

Media type

Chapter 3 of RDA deals with 'describing carriers'. This is a new piece of cataloguing jargon we have to learn. Essentially, carrier information involves what we used to call the format of the item – whether it is a volume or an audio cassette, for example. It also covers a more general form of media type, 'the general type of intermediation device required to view, play, run, etc., the content of a resource' (**RDA 3.2.1.1**). Finally, Chapter 3 deals with the physical description of the item. Putting all this together, we might say that Chapter 3 tells us how to describe the manifestation as a physical object.

RDA 3.2.1.2 gives us a list of general terms that we should use to describe the media type:

1 *audio* – fairly self-explanatory, can be digital or analogue, so media that can be played back on a turntable, cassette player, CD player, MP3 player and so on
2 *computer* – 'media used to store electronic files, designed for use with a computer', including files and discs and material held on a fileserver
3 *microform* – microform, microfilm and so on
4 *microscopic* – media designed to be used with a microscope and so on, for example medical slides and films
5 *projected* – anything designed to be projected on a 'picture film projector, slide projector, or overhead projector. Includes media designed to project both two-dimensional and three-dimensional images'
6 *stereographic* – 'Media used to store pairs of still images, designed for use with a device such as a stereoscope or stereograph viewer to give the effect of three dimensions'
7 *unmediated* – the most common media type in most collections; anything that does not require the use of equipment to view it – so books, pictures and 3D objects such as sculptures and furniture fall into this type
8 *video* – self-explanatory; can be analogue or digital, so includes video cassettes, video discs and DVD videos
9 *other* – after the list, we are instructed to use 'other' for anything that does not fall into types 1–8
10 *unspecified* – if we don't know which category something falls into, we should use unspecified. This caused some discussion among students

in a recent class as to the obstacles in determining media type. Arguably, if we are performing full cataloguing and are given adequate time by our employers to do so, we should be able to determine the media type for any item.

Media type is not a core element, and it will be interesting to see how many cataloguing agencies adopt it.

Carrier type

RDA 3.3 specifies that carrier type is a core element. While media type provides us with a general taxonomy based on the equipment we need to use the item we are cataloguing, carrier type specifies the format:

1 *audio carriers* – audio cartridge; audio cylinder ('use for wax cylinders, wire cylinders, etc.'); audio disc; audio roll ('use for piano rolls, etc.'); audiocassette; audiotape reel; sound-track reel ('use for sound-track films, whether or not they are intended to accompany visual images on film')

2 *computer carriers* – computer card; computer chip cartridge; computer disc; computer disc cartridge; computer tape cartridge; computer tape cassette; computer tape reel; online resource ('use for digital resources that are accessed remotely through a communications network')

3 *microform carriers* – aperture card; microfiche; microfiche cassette; microfilm cartridge; microfilm cassette; microfilm reel; microfilm slip; micro-opaque

4 *microscopic carriers* – microscope slide

5 *projected image carriers* – film cartridge; film cassette; film reel; filmslip; filmstrip; filmstrip cartridge; overhead transparency; slide ('use for photographic slides only; for slides designed to be used with a microscope, use *microscope slide*')

6 *stereographic carriers* – stereograph card; stereograph disc

7 *unmediated carriers* – card; flipchart; roll; sheet; volume (note, as in our example from Appendix M, that a book is entered as 'volume')

8 *video carriers* – video cartridge; videocassette; videotape reel

9 *other* – as in media type, if the item does not fit one of these terms, we
   should enter 'other'

10 *unspecified* – again, if we cannot identify the type, we should enter
   'unspecified'.

Extent

RDA 3.4 tells us that 'Extent is a core element only if the resource is complete
or if the total extent is known. Record subunits only if readily ascertainable
and considered important for identification or selection.'

In our example, this is straightforward, since we have a single-volume book
with clear pagination sequences numbered xxvii and 417.

For some formats, extent is less simple.

RDA 3.4.1.1 defines extent in this way:

> **Extent** reflects the number and type of units and/or subunits making up a resource.
> A **unit** is a physical or logical constituent of a resource (e.g. a volume,
> audiocassette, film reel, or a map or digital file).
> A **subunit** is a physical or logical subdivision of a unit (e.g. a page of a volume, a
> frame of a microfiche, or a record in a digital file).

Examples given include:

- 100 slides
- 1 film reel
- 1 online resource
- 1 computer disc (8 audio files)
- 1 filmstrip (28 frames).

It is not made explicit why in the example in Appendix M the entry is xvii,
417 pages, instead of 1 volume (xvii, 417 pages), so we are left to assume the
standard convention that unless we are told otherwise, we assume the
resource is a standard book.

There are separate instructions for cartographic resources (**RDA 3.4.2**),
notated music (**RDA 3.4.3**), still images (**RDA 3.4.4**) and three-dimensional
forms (**RDA 3.4.6**). In our example, we are dealing with **RDA 3.4.5**, extent of

text. The procedure is essentially the same as in AACR2, although it is important to note that we no longer use the abbreviation 'p.' but write 'page' or 'pages' in full. This is a change that can be made using a global edit on most library management systems.

Practice note

It is important to remember that in AACR2, 'p.' can stand for the singular or the plural, so if you carry out a global edit changing all instances of 'p.' to 'pages' you will have to run a second global edit changing all instances of '1 pages' to '1 page'.

Another change is from **AACR2 2.5B4** in which misleading misnumbered pages could be entered in the form '48 [i.e. 96] p.'. As part of RDA's move away from the use of Latin, we are instructed in **RDA 3.4.5.5** to use the form '48, that is 96 pages'. Again, this is a change that can be made retrospectively using a global edit facility, if so desired.

Dimensions

RDA 3.5 describes how we should deal with the dimensions of the item we are cataloguing. As we can see from our example, there is no change for books, where we give the height in centimetres, '27 cm', always rounding up, 'e.g. if the height measures 17.2 centimetres, record *18 cm*'. As we always discuss in class, this is important for any future library moves – it is no good maximizing on shelving space only to discover that some of the books are a couple of millimetres too tall for their new shelf.

RDA 3.5.1.4.14 instructs us to give the height of a volume in millimetres if it is less than 10 centimetres tall. We should give the height x width if the width is either greater than the height or is less than half the height.

In short, there is no change from AACR2 as far as books are concerned.

Practice note

It is interesting that dimensions is not a core element, since it provides useful information for library planning (shelving moves) and is helpful when items

are misshelved or go missing – always useful to know if you are looking for a standard-sized, over-sized or small item. It is advisable to think very carefully before deciding against recording the dimensions of items on the catalogue.

There are several other aspects of the physical item covered in Chapter 3, including base material such as paper, parchment, skin (**RDA 3.6**); applied material, such as acrylic, ink, tempera (**RDA 3.7**); mount, such as wood, Bristol board (**RDA 3.8**); production method, such as lithograph, photocopy, print (**RDA 3.9**); generation, such as original, master, derivative master (**RDA 3.10**); layout, such as double sided, single sided (**RDA 3.11**); and, interestingly for rare books cataloguers, book format (**RDA 3.12**).

Contact information

Chapter 4 deals with recording information for acquisitions such as availability (**RDA 4.2**) and restrictions on access (**RDA 4.4**). In our example from Appendix M, we can see the application of **RDA 4.3**, contact information.

The basic instruction at **RDA 4.3.1.3** is to 'Record contact information for a publisher or distributor if it is considered to be important for acquisition or access' and we can see in our example this is the publisher's website, www.lu.com.

Practice note

Most libraries already have procedures in place for recording this type of information, and indeed most of the information covered in Chapter 4. It is unusual for it to be recorded in the bibliographic record – links die, suppliers change and generally acquisitions librarians are only too aware of the complications involved in tracking down a resource and so are cautious of giving library users information which, although accurate at the time of entry, may quickly go out of date. It may be the case that the library has acquired the item from a supplier that is not open to members of the public. Before implementing this practice, it is important to check that it is helpful to your end users and the acquisitions team.

Content type

RDA 6.10 identifies content type as a core element. We are given the following choices, and should use as many as apply:

1 *cartographic dataset* – intended to be processed by a computer
2 *cartographic image* – maps, views, atlases and so on
3 *cartographic moving image* – including satellite images
4 *cartographic tactile image* – 'intended to be perceived through touch as a still image in two dimensions'
5 *cartographic tactile three-dimensional form* – 'intended to be perceived through touch as a three-dimensional form'
6 *cartographic three-dimensional form* – globes, relief models and so on
7 *computer dataset* – such as numeric data
8 *computer program* – includes applications and operating systems
9 *notated movement* – for 'movement intended to be perceived visually'
10 *notated music* – 'all forms other than those intended to be perceived through touch'
11 *performed music* – includes musical performances and computer-generated music
12 *sounds* – other than language or music – e.g. natural sounds, like birdsong
13 *spoken word* – 'language in audible form' including readings and oral histories
14 *still image* – drawings, paintings, photographs and so on
15 *tactile image* – 'intended to be perceived through touch in two dimensions'
16 *tactile music* – including Braille music
17 *tactile notated movement* – for 'movement intended to be perceived through touch'
18 *tactile text* – including Braille text
19 *tactile three-dimensional form* – for 'forms intended to be perceived through touch'
20 *text* – most common in most collections, all forms, other than those 'intended to be perceived through touch'
21 *three-dimensional form* – including sculpture, models, objects and holograms

22 *three-dimensional moving image* – including 3-D motion pictures

23 *two-dimensional moving image* – including film and video

24 *other* – where the content cannot be described by one of the terms at 1-23, we should enter 'other'

25 *unspecified* – where we cannot determine the content type, we should enter 'unspecified'.

For our example from Appendix M, the entry is straightforward: as a book, the content type is 'text'.

Language of the content

RDA 7.12 sets out fairly straightforward instructions for recording the language of the content. In our example from Appendix M, it seems a bit over the top to record 'In English' since the normal assumption would be that items in a largely English-language collection were in English unless otherwise specified. MARC catalogue records would already be coded eng to denote their language.

However, **RDA 7.12.1.3** includes some useful examples of language notes, which are familiar from AACR2, such as

Latin text; parallel English translation

Some items in English, some in French

Latin with English marginalia

Dubbed into English

Illustrative content

Chapter 7 is also the section of RDA that deals with illustrations. In the draft from which we are working, this has been missed out, although the Library of Congress record includes 'ill.' in the physical description area.

Illustrations are dealt with in the same way as **AACR2 2.5C**, although it is important to note that where in AACR2 we are instructed to use the term 'ill.' RDA specifies that we use the term 'illustrations'. Older records can be updated using a global edit on most library management systems.

Practice note

As with the change from 'p.' to 'pages', if you perform a global edit changing 'ill.' to 'illustrations' you will have to perform a second global edit to change all cases containing '1 illustrations' to '1 illustration'.

The option at **AACR2 2.5C2** to use more specific terms has been preserved, although, again, RDA does not want us to use abbreviations, as shown in Table 6.2.

Table 6.2 How items specified in AACR2 2.5C2 are treated in RDA 7.15.1.3		
AACR2 2.5C2		**RDA 7.15.1.3**
[not specified]		charts
coats of arms	remains	coats of arms
facsims.	now	facsimiles
forms	remains	forms
genealogical tables	remains	genealogical tables
[not specified]		graphs
[not specified]		illuminations
maps	remains	maps
music	remains	music
[not specified]		photographs
plans	remains	plans
ports.	now	portraits
[not specified]		samples

Cases where **AACR2 2.5C2** did not specify a particular type of illustration were covered by the instruction: 'If none of these terms adequately describes the illustrations, use another term as appropriate.'

Similarly, **RDA 7.15.1.3** and **7.15.1.4** instruct us: 'If none of the terms listed is appropriate or sufficiently specific' we should 'record details of the illustrative content if they are considered to be important for identification or selection'.

Practice note

The usual caveat applies – if you perform a global edit, remember to run a second global edit to catch all the single illustrations that have been pluralized – e.g. change '1 coats of arms' to '1 coat of arms'.

RDA 7.17.1.3 allows us to record the colour of the content. Again, abbreviations are out, as shown in Table 6.3.

Table 6.3 *How items specified in AACR2 2.5C are treated in RDA 7.17.1.3*		
AACR2 2.5C		**RDA 7.17.1.3**
col.	now	colour
some col.	now	some colour
Chiefly col.	now	chiefly colour

RDA does not specify, but we may assume that cataloguers in the USA may use the American English spelling 'color'.

Again, these changes can be carried out retrospectively using a global edit facility on the library management system.

Supplementary content

RDA 7.16 deals with supplementary content such as an index, bibliography or appendix. As we can see in our example record, it is a case of making a note such as 'Includes bibliography and index'.

In the existing Library of Congress record, the cataloguer has chosen to express this as 'Includes bibliographical references (p. 385–405) and index'. This reflects a stylistic difference on the part of the cataloguer rather than a change between AACR2 and RDA.

Creator

Chapter 19 deals with 'persons, families and corporate bodies associated with a work'.

Creator (**RDA 19.2**) is a core element. We are not instructed on those rare cases where the creator is not apparent and cannot be traced.

Fortunately, our example is straightforward: there is only one person associated with this book: its author, Arlene Taylor.

Whereas AACR2 required us to identify a main entry for the work, RDA requires us only to identify access points. **RDA 18.15** sets out the following important definitions:

The term **access point** refers to a name, term, code, etc., under which information pertaining to a specific person, family, or corporate body will be found.

The term **preferred access point** refers to an access point representing a person, family, or corporate body that is constructed using the preferred name for that person, family, or corporate body.

RDA 9.2 instructs us how to record personal names, including the preferred name for the person, which is a core element. Just as AACR2 sets out headings for person, **RDA 9.2** tells us how to construct name headings.

However, in practice, we can assume that most cataloguing agencies will continue to use the Library of Congress Name Authority File at http://authorities.loc.gov/, and will only have recourse to form their own headings for personal names and corporate bodies when a heading has not yet made it onto the Library of Congress system. Indeed, we can see from our example that the Name Authority File has been used to establish the form of heading.

Related work

One of the hopes for RDA is that it will allow us to create more links between records on our catalogues. RDA Chapter 25 sets out guidelines on how this can be done.

RDA 25.1.1.1 tells us that 'A **related work** is a work related to the work represented by a preferred access point (e.g. an adaptation, commentary, supplement, sequel, or part of a larger work)'. **RDA 25.1.1.2** tells us that we can 'Take information on related works from any source'. Examples in **RDA 25.1.1.3** include:

Review of
Commentary in
Contains:
Finding aid:
Supplement to:
Continues:

At the time of writing this is all too new to discuss authoritatively in any depth. We await the national libraries' trials and the policy decisions from the large consortia like OCLC and COPAC.

Our example from Appendix M is somewhat pedestrian, in that its related work is a series added entry, something that was possible under AACR2. Indeed, the Library of Congress record has made exactly the same link. (The use of MARC field 440 simply reflects the record's creation before the change in Summer 2009 to using the 830 field for this type of entry, and has nothing to do with the move from AACR2 to RDA.)

Other examples in Appendix M include a video recording, which we are told is a 'Remake based on the screenplay written by Roy Moore in 1974'.

Conclusion

Having worked through this example, it should be clear that although there have been some big changes, most notably the move away from having a main entry and added entries, much of RDA is familiar to us from its predecessor AACR2. As more and more examples become available through the national libraries and cataloguing consortia, RDA will become more familiar to us and it will be easier to implement in our own libraries.

7

MARC 21

What is MARC 21?

The idea to use computers for cataloguing was developed by the Library of Congress from the 1950s. Various studies were carried out, resulting in the Machine Readable Cataloging (MARC) project; from 1966 Library of Congress MARC data was sent out to 16 libraries on tape (Chan, 2007). A similar initiative took place in the UK under the auspices of the British National Bibliography, and such was the success on both sides of the Atlantic that in 1968 the projects came together to form the MARCII format, an attempt to produce a standard Anglo-American format (Bowman, 2007).

This attempt was only partially successful, and during the next 25 years over 50 different MARC formats developed across the world, including UKMARC and USMARC. Eventually, in 2001 the British Library ceased use and maintenance of the UKMARC format and adopted the harmonized US and Canadian format, MARC 21 (Bowman, 2007).

Lois Mai Chan (2007) identifies five current types of MARC 21 formats:

- MARC 21 for bibliographic data
- MARC 21 for authority data
- MARC 21 for classification data
- MARC 21 for holdings data
- MARC 21 for community information.

We have already looked at MARC 21 for authority data. This chapter considers MARC 21 for bibliographic data, which is used by many libraries for their catalogue records.

Essentially, MARC 21 for bibliographic data exists to provide a structure for catalogue records. The MARC 21 website describes it as a 'communication format' – it is a structure in which data from one computerized catalogue can be shared with another computerized catalogue.

Catalogue format, not cataloguing code

It is vital to understand that the MARC format provides the structure while other cataloguing codes provide the rules. Although the MARC website provides lots of useful examples, MARC 21 does not set out to be a cataloguing code. This is highlighted in the introduction to the format:

> The **content** of the data elements that comprise a MARC record is usually defined by standards outside the formats. Examples are the *International Standard Bibliographic Description* (ISBD), *Anglo-American Cataloguing Rules*, *Library of Congress Subject Headings* (LCSH), or other cataloging rules, subject thesauri, and classification schedules used by the organization that creates a record.

This chapter is designed to be used alongside MARC 21's website and AACR2, which is still the main cataloguing code used in libraries. A section at the end of the chapter deals with the new fields introduced to MARC 21 in February 2010 to accommodate RDA.

The structure of a MARC record

MARC 21 records can be conveniently discussed in three parts:

- *record leader* – described as 'data elements that primarily provide information for the processing of the record, the data elements contain numbers or coded values'
- *directory* – showing the format's roots in the days of magnetic tape, the directory consists of 'a series of entries that contain the tag, length, and starting location of each variable field within a record'
- *fields* – into which we enter our bibliographic information – access points and descriptive cataloguing.

It is probably clear from this brief overview that we need not concern ourselves here with the first two elements of the record: both leader and directory are performing data coding functions and most library management systems are set up to complete them automatically.

In this chapter, we will look at the main fields that we use to record our bibliographic information. First, let us look at the structure of a typical MARC field.

All MARC fields consist of a three-digit **tag**. The most common include:

100   Main entry – personal name
245   Title statement
260   Publication, distribution, etc. (imprint)
300   Physical description

Each tag makes use of **indicators** and **subfields**.

Indicators are a further two digits that can be used to provide more information about the tag or define it in some way. For example, in the 100 tag, the first indicator is used to tell us whether the name is entered under a forename (indicator 0), surname (indicator 1, the most common) or family name (indicator 3), and the second indicator is left blank. In the 245 tag, the indicators perform a different function, but still give us information about the tag: the first indicator tells us whether there is a title main entry (indicator 0) or title added entry (indicator 1) and the second indicator allows for up to nine characters at the start of the title to be ignored for filing purposes (indicator 0-9).

Subfields can be identified by their **delimiter**, which is usually a lower case letter. Depending on the library management system you are using, this will be preceded by a pipe-mark (|) or a dollar sign ($). Each subfield delimiter plays its own role within the tag, so, for example, in the 245 field, $a is the title and $c statement of responsibility.

Main entries and added entries revisited

MARC currently follows AACR2 in observing the practice of having main entries and added entries to provide access points for records. It also has fields that provide purely descriptive information, such as the 300 field, which is for physical description.

Of course, many library management systems allow for free-text searching on any field, or, indeed, of the whole record, and RDA is proposing different ways to deal with access points. At the time of writing (Autumn 2011), MARC maintains main entry fields which start with the digit 1 and added entry fields which start with either digit 7 or digit 8:

100	Main entry – personal name
700	Added entry – personal name
110	Main entry – corporate name
710	Main entry – corporate name
111	Main entry – meeting name [conference heading]
711	Main entry – meeting name [conference heading]
130	Main entry – uniform title
830	Series added entry – uniform title

Punctuation

Mostly MARC 21 follows standard AACR2/ISBD punctuation, but there are some exceptions to this, so always check the input conventions section for the field on the MARC website.

Practice note

You also need to be aware of how your own library management system treats MARC codes and punctuation – some have a legacy of embedded or system-generated punctuation, so always check a new system to see how your records display. UKMARC did not require standard punctuation to be input, so from 1998 onwards, when MARC 21 began to be implemented in the UK, punctuation formed a thorny issue for libraries and library management system (LMS) vendors alike.

Common MARC 21 fields
100, 700 – Entries for person

The use of Name Authority Files (NAF) maintained by the Library of Congress and other NACO contributors simplifies entry for most names, which can usually be transcribed from the NAF.

That said, you need to know how to enter name headings, since there will always be instances of names that do not have entries in the NAF. Indeed, you may even become one of the cataloguers responsible for creating new NAF headings.

Indicators

The first indicator in the 100 and 700 fields indicates the type of personal name element, whether it is:

Forename – 0
Surname – 1
Family name – 3

The 100 field does not use the second indicator. In the 700 field, an indicator of 2 indicates an analytical entry.

The most common subfields are:

$a personal name
$d dates associated with a name

100 1_$aElgar, Edward,$d1857-1934

You can find further examples in the section in Chapter 4 'Name authority control'.

110, 710 – Entries for corporate body

As with personal names, the entry for corporate bodies is covered by the Library of Congress and NACO Name Authority Files. However, it is important to know how to construct headings for corporate bodies in case you come across one that has not yet made it into the NAF.

Indicators

The second indicator is undefined, and there are only three options for the first indicator:

Inverted name – 0
Jurisdiction name – 1
Name in direct order – 2

The inverted name is very uncommon.

There are many subfields available for use, but by far the most common are:

$a Corporate name or jurisdiction name as entry element
$b Subordinate unit

Logically enough, $a is non-repeatable, but you can repeat $b as often as necessary.

In these examples, the name is given in direct order, with the second example having a subordinate body (the Institute of English Studies is part of the University of London).

110   2_$aUnited Nations
110   2_$aUniversity of London.$bInstitute of English Studies

Here we see the correct format for a jurisdiction with subordinate body:

110   1_$aGreat Britain.$bHome Office
110   1_$aUnited States.$bArmy

You can find further examples in the section 'Name authority control' in Chapter 4.

111, 711 – Entries for conferences and other meetings

As we know from AACR2, a conference or meeting is really a specific form of corporate body, and so it should come as no surprise that the indicators in the 111 and 711 fields function in exactly the same way as in the 110 and 710 fields. The second indicator is undefined, and there are only three options for the first indicator:

Inverted name – 0
Jurisdiction name – 1
Name in direct order – 2

Again, the inverted name is very uncommon.

Of the many subfields available, the most common are:

$a – Meeting/conference or jurisdiction name
$n – Number of meeting (formed as per AACR2 as an ordinal number)
$d – Date of meeting (year only, as per AACR2)
$c – Location of meeting/conference

AACR2 punctuation is followed, so if we take Bowman's Pineapple example, International Pineapple Symposium (3rd : 1998 : Pattaya, Thailand) we can enter it in MARC fields as:

111   2_$aInternational Pineapple Symposium$n(3rd
:$d1998 : $cPattaya, Thailand)

Note that unlike most punctuation, which is entered to *precede* the subfield code, the opening bracket is entered *after* the $n.

Conferences are covered by the Library of Congress and NACO Authority File. However, coverage is much less comprehensive than that for personal names, so you need to know how to form conference headings yourself.

130 – Uniform title (main entry)

This field is used when the uniform title is to be the main entry for the record. The MARC manual states: 'Main entry under a uniform title is used when a work is entered directly under title and the work has appeared under varying titles, necessitating that a particular title be chosen to represent the work.'

So, if a work has no person of chief responsibility and is not the emanation of a corporate body, *and* has appeared under varying titles, we should choose the 130 field rather than the 240 field for the uniform title.

Indicators

The second indicator is not used, and the first indicator indicates the number of non-filing characters from 0 to 9.

There are many subfields available, of which the most common are:

$a – uniform title
$l – language
$s – version

As you may have predicted, many of the works that require main entry under uniform title are religious, such as the Bible and the Koran, hence the usefulness of $s:

    130   0_$aBible.$lEnglish.$sAuthorized.
    130   0_$aKoran.$lEnglish.

However, some other important works in the literary canon require main entry under uniform title:

    130   0_$aBeowulf.$lEnglish.
    130   0_$aLancelot du Lac.$lEnglish.

240 – Uniform title (where there is main entry under 100, 110 or 111)

Most uniform titles have an author or other person of chief responsibility, or are the emanation of a corporate body (or conference). Where there is a 100,

110 or 111 entry to be made for the item in your hand, you can enter the uniform title in the 240 field.

Indicators

The first indicator is used to decide whether the uniform title needs to be displayed or not:

If we don't want to print or display it – 0
If we do want to print or display it – 1

Because we generally only create uniform titles to aid our users in finding books with varying titles, there is an almost 100% chance we will want to display the uniform title. It is hard to think of an example of a record requiring first indicator 0.

The second indicator is used to indicate non-filing characters, and can be 0–9.

The subfields available are the same as those for the 130 field.

For clarity of comparison with 130 uniform titles, these examples give the main entry and the 240 entry:

```
100     10$aRowling, J. K.
240     10$aHarry Potter and the prisoner of
            Azkaban.$lFrench.
```

```
100     10$aDumas, Alexandre,$d1802-1870.
240     10$aTulipe noire.$lEnglish.
```

Note in the second example that we have not created the heading as 'La tulipe noire'. Although MARC allows for non-filing characters using the second indicator, AACR2 gives the clear instruction at 25.2C1 to 'Omit an initial article (see Initial Articles, appendix E) unless the uniform title is to file under that article (e.g. a title that begins with the name of a person or place)'.

245 – Title and statement of responsibility

The online MARC 21 manual defines the 245 field as follows:

> Title and statement of responsibility area of the bibliographic description of a work.

> Title Statement field consists of the title proper and may also contain the general material designation (medium), remainder of title, other title information, the remainder of the title page transcription, and statement(s) of responsibility. The title proper includes the short title and alternative title, the numerical designation of a part/section and the name of a part/section.

Let us unpack that with reference to some examples, and look at exactly how MARC structures title information.

Indicators

The first indicator is used to establish whether there is a title added entry or not.

Use 1 when the title added entry is the same as the entry in 245. Records without a 1XX entry always have an indicator of 0.

The second indicator is used to indicate the number of non-filing characters at the beginning of the field. These are used for definite and indefinite articles, so in English the most common second indicator is 4 for 'The', but also might be 2 for 'A' or 3 for 'An':

245 10$aMiffy's dream /$cDick Bruna

You can also use this indicator to ignore punctuation at the start of the entry, as in this example from the MARC 21 manual:

245 15$aThe 'winter mind' :$bWilliam Bronk and
    American letters/$cBurt Kimmelman

Practice note

Check your library management system does not have specific requirements with regard to indicators in general and initial punctuation in particular. The filing in some LMS structures is non-standard.

Frequently used subfield codes

As described at the start of the chapter, we use subfield codes to separate the different elements of our entry.

The most frequently used subfield codes in the 245 tag are:

$a – Title
$b – Remainder of title (i.e. 'other title information' in AACR parlance, or 'sub-title')
$c – Statement of responsibility, etc.

If we take this example in AACR2 punctuation:

The war of the unstamped : the movement to repeal the British newspaper tax, 1830-1836 / by Joel H. Wiener

This is entered in MARC as:

245 14$aThe war of the unstamped :$bthe movement to repeal the British newspaper tax, 1830-1836 /$cby Joel H. Wiener

Punctuation

Because MARC is simply a container for AACR2 (and soon RDA), the punctuation remains the same. However, this is where our caveat to think about cataloguing punctuation as something that *precedes* a piece of catalogue data comes into its own. In MARC, the colon that *precedes the remainder of title information* appears *at the end* of the $a subfield, while the oblique that *precedes* the statement of responsibility area appears *at the end* of the $b subfield.

If there is no remainder of title information, $a will not end with a colon, as in this example, where it ends with the oblique that precedes the $c:

245 10$aEssential cataloguing /$cJ. H. Bowman

It is also important to note that none of these fields are repeatable. This does not mean that you can only enter one sub-title or one statement of responsibility. It simply means that you use the subfield code for the first and then use punctuation to indicate the others, as in this example:

245 10$aRadical cataloguing :$bessays at the Front /$cedited by K.R. Roberto; introduction by Sanford Berman

Medium

Another useful non-repeatable subfield is $h, used to record medium. Note the punctuation and the order in which we are instructed to use it:

> In records formulated according to ISBD principles, the medium designator appears in lowercase letters and is enclosed within brackets. It follows the title proper (subfields $a, $n, $p) and precedes the remainder of the title ($b), subsequent titles (in items lacking a collective title), and/or statement(s) of responsibility ($c).

AACR2 uses the term 'General Material Designation (GMD)' for the same concept that MARC terms 'medium' and provides lists of terms to be used at 1.1C1. Note that in the UK we are instructed to use List 1, while in Australia, Canada and the USA we are instructed to use the somewhat longer List 2.

A CD of *The history boys* would be entered:

245 14$aThe history boys$h[sound recording] / $cAlan Bennett

Multipart works

In multipart works use $n to record the number of a part or section of a work and/or $p to record the name of a part or section of a work:

245 10$aPenguin modern poets. $n1,$pLawrence Durrell, Elizabeth Jennings, R. S. Thomas

245 10$aPixar short films collection. $nVolume 1$h[videorecording]

246 – Varying form of title

As publishers become more and more creative with their titles, cataloguers often need to add a different version of the title to aid catalogue users in finding the item.

There are four different actions that can be taken when adding a varying title, and each is denoted by the first indicator:

note made, but no added entry made – 0
note and added entry made – 1
no note made, no added entry made – 2
no note made, but added entry made – 3

The most common examples are 1 and 3 – you want to create an added entry for the variant title. You use indicator 3 when you want to make an added entry, but no note is required to explain why.

The second indicator can be used to explain why you feel the need to record the variant title:

\# – No type specified
0 – Portion of title
1 – Parallel title
2 – Distinctive title
3 – Other title
4 – Cover title
5 – Added title page title
6 – Caption title
7 – Running title
8 – Spine title

So *The Walker book of animal tales* might be given a variant title that is a portion of the title proper:

245 04$aThe Walker book of animal tales
246 30$aBook of animal tales

Since not all searchers will remember that *l8r g8r* is written in text language, we might want to provide a standard English form:

245 10$al8r, g8r /$cLauren Myracle
246 3_$aLater, gator

In both these cases, it should be obvious to anyone reading the catalogue record where the variant title has come from, so there is no need for a note to be generated.

I ♥ my zimmer poses many problems for the cataloguer. It is unlikely that the library management system can process the ♥ symbol and render it searchable, even if the end user knew how to enter it in the search box. Moreover, we all know from the progenitor of all ♥ messages, 'I ♥ NEW YORK', that they can be read two ways, as 'heart' or 'love'. Since the publisher website refers to the title as 'I (Heart) My Zimmer' (Little Brown, 2008), we would suggest the following 245 and 246 entries:

245 10$aI heart my zimmer /$cBill Fallover
246 3_$aI love my zimmer
246 0_$iTitle typeset as:$aI ♥ my zimmer

In this way, we create an entry for the most common reading of ♥ ('heart'). An added entry is created for the alternative reading ('love'), which does not require a note because our reason for doing so (to provide user access) will be obvious to anyone reading the record.

Assuming our library management system can reproduce the ♥ symbol, but cannot render it searchable we create a second 246, which generates a note, but no added entry. Note the use of the $i subfield to display the text of the note. Logically, it appears before the $a, since used together they create the note 'Title typeset as: I ♥ my zimmer'.

A full list of the subfields for the 246 field is available at www.loc.gov/marc/bibliographic/bd246.html.

250 – Edition

This field does not use indicators, and has two very straightforward subfields:

$a – Edition statement
$b – Remainder of edition statement

Punctuation follows AACR2:

250 __$a4th ed.
250 __$aRev. ed.
250 __$aNew ed.
250 __$a12th ed. /$bby David Hayton and Charles Mitchell

260 – Publication, etc.
Indicators

This field has a blank second indicator. The first indicator is used to indicate the sequence of publishing statements:

If this is the earliest publisher, or no information is given, blank first indicator
Not the first, nor the latest publisher, but an 'intervening publisher' – 2
Current publisher – 3

Many libraries choose always to leave the first indicator blank.

It stands to reason that in those libraries that do use this indicator, for modern books the most common indicator is 3.

The most common subfields are:

$a – Place of publication
$b – Name of publisher
$c – Date of publication

Standard ISBD punctuation is followed, so that the $b is preceded by a colon and $c is preceded by a comma. Where the $a is repeated, it is preceded by a semi-colon; where $b is repeated, it is preceded by a semi-colon:

260 3_$aLondon :$bSweet & Maxwell,$c2005

260 __$aMedford, N.J. :$bInformation Today,$c2007

260 3_$aLondon ;$aBoston ;$bButterworths,$c1990

300 – Physical description

This field does not use indicators.

The most common subfields in use are:

$a – Extent

$b – Other physical details, such as illustrations

$c – Dimensions, usually expressed in centimetres or millimetres

Punctuation is as per AACR2, as in the following examples:

300 __$a64 p. : $bill., maps ; $c22 cm.

300 __$a[93] p.: $bill.; $c90 mm.

In this second example, the measurement is given in millimetres because it is less than 10 centimetres (AACR2 2.5D1).

Accompanying material is recorded in $e:

300 __$a95, [9] p. : $bill. ; $c18 cm. + $e1 game (one sheet, fold.)

300 __$a[25] p. : $bchiefly col. ill. ; $c16 cm. + $e1 sound cassette

490 – Series statement

Until Summer 2009 series entries were complicated by the existence of two separate fields – one for series that were traced and one for series that were not. Now this function has been rolled up into one field: 490. The first indicator in this field is used to show whether a series needs a tracing or not:

Series statement, no tracing – 0

Series statement with tracing – 1

The second indicator is not used.

There are several subfields available, of which the most common are:

$a – series statement
$v – volume designator

Punctuation

It is important to note that the brackets used in AACR2 for series statements are not input in MARC. According to the website, 'Parentheses that customarily enclose the series statement are not carried in the machine-readable record. They may be system generated as a display constant associated with the field tag.'

Practice note

Check how your library management system deals with the 490 field. You may have to 'switch on' the automated display of brackets (or ask your systems librarian to do so). Alternatively, you may have to defy MARC and enter brackets manually.

5 – Notes

MARC provides scope for detailed notes to be entered as the cataloguer sees fit. For a full list, see the online manual at www.loc.gov/marc/bibliographic/bd5xx.html.

The most frequently used notes fields are:

500 – General note
501 – With note
504 – Bibliography note
505 – Formatted contents note
520 – Summary, etc.
521 – Target audience note
534 – Original version note
561 – Ownership and custodial history

563 – Binding information

59X – Local notes

500 – General note

Both indicators are undefined, and although there are five subfields, including $6, that can be used for linkage, most cataloguing agencies use only $a.

The manual defines 500 __ $a as 'Note that provides general information for which a specialized note field has not been defined' so the idea is that if you can't find a place in the rest of the 500s where you can enter the note, you can enter it here.

Some libraries don't use other notes fields, preferring to use the 500 field for everything. Even where that is not the case, the range of notes appearing in the field is almost infinite. These examples are all from the MARC manual:

500 __$aIncludes index.

500 __$aTranslated from German.

500 __$aImprint stamped on verso of t.p.

500 __$aBased on a play which originally appeared in France as 'Un peu plus tard, un peu plus tôt'.

500 __$aTable of cases: p. xiii-xvi.

501 – With note

Again, the indicators are undefined, and although there are four subfields, including $6, that can be used for linkage, most cataloguing agencies use only $a.

MARC defines the with note as a 'Note indicating that more than one bibliographical work is contained in the physical item at the time of publishing, release, issue, or execution. The works that are contained in the item usually have distinctive titles and lack a collective title.'

If we are applying MARC strictly and precisely, we should note the key phrase 'at the time of publishing' – if the items have simply been bound together at a later date, they should be entered in binding information (MARC 563) or possibly as a local note, since this information is copy-specific.

The form of entry is straightforward, as exemplified in the MARC manual:

501 __$aWith: The reformed school / John Dury. London : Printed for
R. Wasnothe, [1850].

504 – Bibliography note

This is arguably the most frequently used of all the specific notes fields.

As with most notes fields, the indicators are undefined, and although other
subfields are available, most cataloguing agencies use only $a.

Although cataloguers are free to enter notes in whatever way they feel best
describes the material in hand, the standard formulae for entries in this field
are:

504 __$aBibliography: p.238-239.
504 __$aIncludes bibliographic references.
504 __$aIncludes bibliographies and index.
504 __$aIncludes bibliographic references and index.

505 – Formatted contents note

This is one of the most frequently used notes fields, and allows us to input
individual chapter headings, which can be particularly useful for collections
of short stories by different individuals.

The first indicator can be used to indicate whether the record shows the
complete contents or partial contents:

All contents – 0
Incomplete contents (awaiting the arrival of more item parts) – 1
Partial contents (cataloguer has selected contents to include in the note) – 2

It is important to note that the second indicator is used to indicate whether
the content note is basic (set out as a long string of information at $a) or
whether it is enhanced (using the full range of subfields available):

Only $a used – blank
Full range of subfields used – 1

Many cataloguing agencies use only $a, but use of the other subfields is not uncommon:

$a – formatted contents note
$g – miscellaneous information
$r – statement of responsibility
$t – title
$u – uniform reference identifier
$6 – linkage
$8 – field link and sequence number

Cataloguing agencies using more than $a most commonly use $r and $t, which are repeatable. The following example shows how to enter a contents note using only $a or using $t and $r:

505 0_$aFire / Vikram Seth -- The island / Mark
        Haddon -- Playing with / Geoff Dyer -- Aflame
        in Athens / Victoria Hislop -- A family
        evening / Sebastian Faulks -- The king who
        never spoke / John le Carré -- Into the world
        / Xialu Guo -- Sandcastles : a negotiation /
        William Sutcliffe -- Last / Ali Smith -- Long
        time, no see / Lionel Shriver -- Dog days /
        Jeannette Winterson -- Afterword / Oxfam

505 01$tFire /$rVikram Seth -- $tThe island /$rMark
        Haddon -- $tPlaying with /$rGeoff Dyer --
        $tAflame in Athens /$rVictoria Hislop -- $tA
        family evening /$rSebastian Faulks -- $tThe
        king who never spoke /$rJohn le Carré -- $tInto
        the world /$rXialu Guo -- $tSandcastles: a
        negotiation /$rWilliam Sutcliffe -- $tLast
        /$rAli Smith -- $tLong time, no see /$rLionel
        Shriver -- $tDog days /$rJeannette Winterson --
        $tAfterword /$rOxfam

520 – Summary, etc.

520 is used for abstracts, reviews and summaries, and unlike most notes fields, uses its first indicator to denote the type of content in the field:

Summary – blank
Subject – 0
Review – 1
Scope and content – 2
Abstract – 3
Content advice – 4

The second indicator is undefined.

Although there are eight subfields available, most cataloguing agencies use only $a.

Many cataloguing agencies do not use the indicator. Where they are in use, the beginning cataloguer may need to differentiate between summaries and abstracts, as in these examples:

520 __$aProvides contact information about drug
        treatment and care services in England and the
        Channel Islands. Services are arranged by
        county, town and type.

520 3_$aThe present paper describes a patient who
        exhibited 'Alice in Wonderland' (AIW) syndrome
        as well as lilliputian hallucinations. The
        patient regularly consumed a cough syrup that
        contained dihydrocodein phosphate and dl-
        methylephedrine hydrochloride over 3 years. At
        the age of 46, he developed AIW syndrome. The
        patient ingested a large dose of triazolam and
        exhibited delirium. Even after the
        disappearance of symptoms associated with AIW
        syndrome and delirium, the patient continued
        to experience lilliputian hallucinations. We

> believe that these hallucinations were caused
> by some of the components of the cough syrup.

We might observe that the abstract is longer and more detailed than the summary, and has been written using as many terms as the cataloguer can imagine that users might choose as search terms in a free-text search. In contrast, the summary is simply two brief sentences that inform the catalogue user of the nature of the publication.

The option to provide review notes is one that can seem obscure to beginning cataloguers. It is used mainly by specialist research collections, especially where analytical cataloguing of book chapters and journal articles is undertaken:

> 520 1_ $aReview of 'Ask Alice' and the issues it
>   raised about teenage drug use

With RDA's emphasis on how works relate to each other, we may see an upsurge in libraries using 520 1_ notes.

521 Target audience note

It will come as no surprise that the 521 note field is particularly useful for libraries that hold a lot of children's literature.

The first indicator is used to indicate different levels of audience:

> General audience note – blank
> Reading grade level – 0
> Interest age level – 1
> Interest grade level – 2
> Special audience characteristics – 3
> Motivation/interest level – 3

The second indicator is undefined.

Although there are five subfields available, most cataloguing agencies use only $a.

Many school libraries do not have library management systems based on

MARC cataloguing, and so instances of reading grade level notes in MARC are not as commonplace as we might expect. However, searching on Worldcat for well known children's titles, we can see that the interest grade level is used frequently by contributing cataloguing agencies.

If we are cataloguing in a library management system that is coded for pure MARC, we can enter information in a coded form and a note will be generated automatically, as in this example from the MARC manual:

Numbered information in subfield $a pertains to the age level at which the item will most likely be of interest. The value is used to generate the display constant Interest age level:

521 1_$a008-012.

[The item is of interest to those aged 8-12.]

In practice, many systems cannot deal (or have not been set up to deal) with this form of coding to generate the note, and so cataloguers have to enter the note manually:

521 1_$aInterest age level: 8-12.

It is not uncommon to see audience notes that veer away from the standardized form of entry, as in this example:

521 1_$a'Ages 3-8'—Front flap of dustjacket.

Practice note

It is important to be clear how this note field has been set up on your library management system, and, if it has been set up to allow for free-text input, to check the input conventions in your local cataloguing manual by looking at examples on the catalogue.

534 – Original version note

Most cataloguing agencies record the original publication of an item when it is recorded on the item itself, since it is a useful piece of information for users. Only recently I was putting together a workshop on feminist creative writing and had cause to look up the original publication date of Virginia Woolf's *A room of one's own*. Although, arguably, we might turn to Wikipedia for such queries, I found the date I was looking for very quickly from the reliable source of a catalogue record in the British Library.

Many agencies do not use the 534 to record this information, but instead enter it as a general note in the 500 field.

Practice note

If you are working on a new catalogue, check if your library uses the 500 field or the 534 field to record this information.

Both indicators are undefined.

There are 17 subfields available for this field (perhaps one of the reasons so many agencies prefer the 500 field). Please see www.loc.gov/marc/bibliographic/bd534.html for the complete list.

The most commonly used subfields are:

$p – Introductory phrase
$c – Publication of the original
$t – title of the original

534 __$pOriginally published:$cLondon : Little, Brown, 1998.

534 __$pOriginally published as:$tEchoes from the macabre,$cLondon : Victor Gollancz, 1976.

561 – Ownership and custodial history

There has been a growth in the interest in provenance research over the last 10–15 years, and more and more libraries are recording the provenance of items in their special collections.

The first indicator can be used to indicate the privacy level of the information:

No information as to privacy – blank
Private information – 0
Not private – 1

However, many libraries are wary of relying on computer coding to hide private information from public display, and enter only public information in this field, maintaining separate files for information that could be sensitive, such as the name and address of a donor.

The second indicator is undefined.

There are five subfields available, but most cataloguing agencies use only $a.

Here are some real-world examples of provenance notes:

561 __$aInscription: Charles Young, July 1930.
561 __$aContains book label on front pastedown: De la Bibliotheque de M. Dumeril.
561 __$aFrom the library of Sir John Rotton, bequeathed 1926.
561 __$aInscriptions on title-page verso and several other blank leaves: 'Thomas Moore'.

If the examples had been taken from a library that chose to use the first indicator to denote the privacy level of the information, they would be coded 561 1_.

563 – Binding information

Binding information is often recorded, especially by special collections departments. Like most notes fields, the indicators are undefined. Although there are six subfields available, most cataloguing agencies use only $a.

Information can be as detailed or as general as the library requires:

563 __$aBuckram binding.

563 __$aModern buckram binding; edges red.

563 __$aBlue cloth binding

563 __$aNavy blue cloth binding, gilt text on upper board and spine,
  top edge stained blue.

59X – Local notes

Local notes are implemented in libraries for many different reasons. The most common is probably to record information about the local copy that, for whatever reason, cannot be entered into the holdings information, as in these real-world examples:

590 __$aTitle-page and first few pages slightly damaged.

590 __$aThe whole volume has suffered some water damage.

590 __$aLacking the 6 advertisement leaves.

Practice note

If your cataloguing agency is entering into a cataloguing consortium for the first time or sharing records in a less formal way, take care to discuss what will happen with local notes – will they be excluded from your data sharing, or will you accept each others' local notes and amend them as necessary? Different agencies use the 59X fields for very different purposes and you don't want to confuse them.

The impact of RDA

In February 2010, Update 11 to MARC 21 for Bibliographic Data implemented changes to accommodate the new information RDA would like us to record. A document entitled *RDA in MARC* was published on the MARC website at www.loc.gov/marc/RDAinMARC29.html summarizing changes in the following areas:

RDA Content Types
RDA Media Types

RDA Carrier Types
New MARC Authority Fields for Name Attributes
New MARC Authority and Bibliographic Fields for Work and Expression

Several of the new MARC fields represent important shifts in the way that we catalogue. Since most cataloguing agencies will not be in a position to implement the new fields until 2011/12, it seemed more appropriate to discuss them in Chapter 5, which deals with the introduction of RDA in general terms. In this way, we can discuss the new fields in the context of the new cataloguing principles they represent in RDA.

8

Practical cataloguing: bringing it all together

When we first started to write this book, we thought that the gap in the market was for a text that would describe how to catalogue from start to finish, using the new cataloguing standard, RDA.

In practice, RDA was not as close to implementation as we thought, and instead we have written a book about cataloguing standards in transition, and cataloguing practice, consequently, in flux.

So what does practical cataloguing look like during this time of change? There were two surveys of cataloguer attitudes towards RDA in 2010, one on each side of the Atlantic, and they each asked slightly different questions.

The North American survey conducted by Elaine Sanchez (Texas State University San-Marcos) attracted responses from 668 people, with 49.2% (326 respondents) working in college or university libraries and 22.5% (149 respondents) employed by public libraries (Sanchez, 2010). The survey attracted responses from all over the world, but less than 4% were from outside North America.

Sanchez has said 'I'm a cataloguer, not a survey-designer or statistician' and she invited others to perform secondary analysis on her data (Sanchez, 2011). As a non-statistician, she collected data on one of the most difficult areas for people to describe – their feelings – asking the question 'Please select the word or words that most closely match your personal feelings toward RDA' and eliciting a response that showed 'Uncertainty' out in the lead, with 388 people selecting it as (one of) their emotion(s) (Figure 8.1 overleaf).

Another interesting finding in this survey comes in response to the question 'Please rate your knowledge of Cataloging on the Semantic Web, using the scale of 1–5, with 1 as the lowest: '1 "No 'knowledge"'' and 5 as the highest

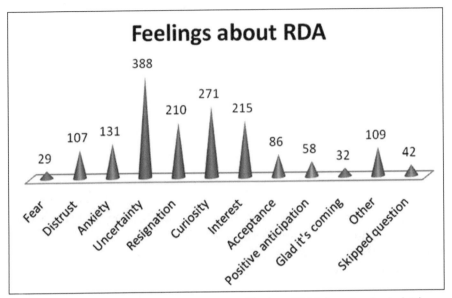

Figure 8.1 *Feelings about RDA* (Source: generated by Anne Welsh from Sanchez's data)

'Expert knowledge' (Figure 8.2). In the survey 258 respondents rated themselves at 1, while another 210 skipped the question.

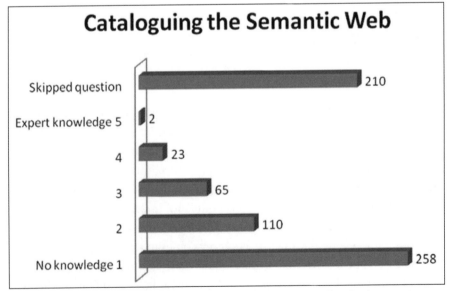

Figure 8.2 *Extent of knowledge about cataloguing on the Semantic Web of respondents to survey by Sanchez* (Source: generated by Anne Welsh from Sanchez's data)

These two questions in Sanchez's survey have captured a snapshot of cataloguers who feel wary about change and under-confident in the knowledge needed to embrace that change.

In the UK, CILIP's Cataloguing & Indexing Group (CIG) carried out a survey in order to get a picture of cataloguers' perceived training needs. The results were presented by Alan Danskin at the appropriately named CIG Conference 2010: 'Every cloud has a silver lining? Changes in cataloguing in "interesting times"'. Alan's slides are available on the CIG website (www.cilip.org.uk/get-involved/special-interest-groups/cataloguing-indexing/Pages/default.aspx).

The UK survey elicited only 78 responses. Again, the majority of respondents worked in academic (58%) or public (14%) libraries, although government libraries came a close third (10%).

Nearly all (90%) respondents catalogue in MARC format, with 100% cataloguing according to AACR2, although some were supplementing it with other standards, including DCRM(B), *AACR2 for Cartographic Materials* and ISAD(G) (Figures 8.3 and 8.4).

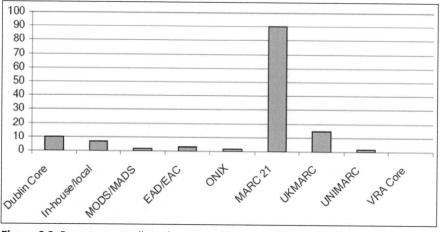

Figure 8.3 *Formats or encoding schemes used by respondents to CILIP's CIG survey (Source: Danskin, 2010)*

Further questions elicited the amount of time that people felt their organizations would allocate to training, the type of training needed, and the costs they felt they or their organizations would be willing to pay for the training. One interesting slide showed that less than 25% of respondents would be 'interested in assisting CIG to offer RDA training to other

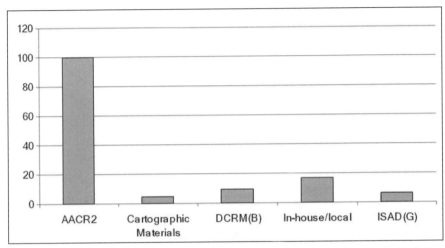

Figure 8.4 *Cataloguing rules or metadata instructions used by respondents to CILIP's CIG survey* (Source: Danskin, 2010)

institutions', although no subsidiary data is offered offering reasons for this, so we are left wondering whether the other respondents lack time, interest or, as indicated by Sanchez's survey, confidence in their own knowledge to assist with this training.

One thing is clear from these two surveys: cataloguers on both sides of the Atlantic feel they are living in 'interesting times'.

Key activities for cataloguing managers

With strategists from the Library of Congress and the British Library predicting that if RDA is implemented in their organizations the change from AACR2 to RDA will not begin until January 2013 at the earliest, it is clear that those responsible for cataloguing policy in other libraries would be best advised to watch and wait. These are some of the places to look for information:

- The Library of Congress's web pages on testing RDA at www.loc.gov/bibliographic-future/rda/. The report of the tests was released in Summer 2011, and shortly afterwards the Library of Congress made a statement on its decisions for implementation and/or national leadership for the new cataloguing code.

- British Library Metadata Standards at www.bl.uk/bibliographic/catstandards.html. The British Library is also likely to publish further information following the report on the US national tests. Normally official British Library reports are also posted to the lis-ukbibs mailing list (https://www.jiscmail.ac.uk/cgi-bin/webadmin?A0=lis-ukbibs).
- The Joint Steering Committee for the Development of RDA at www.rda-jsc.org/. News from the JSC is posted on its website and to the RDA discussion list, www.rda-jsc.org/rdadiscuss.html (a fairly high-volume discussion list). There are useful presentations, including some with detailed comparisons between AACR2 and RDA at www.rda-jsc.org/rdapresentations.html.
- AUTOCAT. This continues to be the main e-mail list for discussions of all sorts relating to cataloguing, including RDA – https://listserv.syr.edu/scripts/wa.exe?A0=AUTOCAT (N.B. This is an extremely high-volume mailing list).
- CILIP's Cataloguing and Indexing Group. The group posts news to its blog, including news about RDA and relevant trainings and events – http://communities.cilip.org.uk/blogs/catalogueandindex/default.aspx.
- The American Library Association. The ALA maintains a list of US-based interest groups relating to cataloguing and other technical services (through the Association for Library Collections & Technical Services) at http://connect.ala.org/taxonomy/term/9366 ALCTS sometimes runs free web fora on topics relating to RDA.
- The RDA Toolkit. This has its own website at www.rdatoolkit.org/, which includes news, although the co-publishers are very diligent about posting information to AUTOCAT and RDA-L.
- *Cataloging & Classification Quarterly*, published by Taylor & Francis. This is the main journal for cataloguing; in 2011 most issues were full of articles on RDA.

Those responsible for cataloguing teams can also think about running awareness-raising sessions. As should have been clear from the rest of this book, the move to RDA is part of a general move towards linked data and the semantic web, and it is helpful to run sessions for staff in which they can learn about the concepts and new terminologies. Topics covered might include:

- AACR2 as one set of rules employed to achieve general cataloguing principles, and part of a long history from Panizzi and Cutter to date
- FRBR, its attributes, entities and relationship to the tradition of library cataloguing, as well as its role as the foundation for RDA
- linked data and the open bibliographic data movement
- the library catalogue and the deep web (Karen Coyle publishes widely and frequently on the difficulty of accessing library data from search engines, which we know is the most common way that students (and others) begin searches)
- the semantic web.

There are good quality, free videos and screencasts available for most of these topics. It can be productive to watch them together, stopping the recording at appropriate points to discuss issues raised, and/or to add information about local practice.

At the CILIP Executive Briefing on RDA, Celine Carty shared her experience running sessions like these at the University of Cambridge. She recounted how the session on AACR2 and RDA was so over-subscribed that she had to run it three times, even although she warned staff that a high proportion of the slides were literally showing the difference between records in AACR2 and RDA, and even although the majority of staff were not cataloguers.

Key activities for cataloguers

Although at UCL we teach ten weeks of practicals based on AACR2 and MARC 21 (alongside lectures on a wider range of cataloguing topics), we are always at pains to point out to students that what we are teaching in practicals is not simply a set of rules to be applied, but 'general cataloguing principles as exemplified by the dominant cataloguing standard of the day'. The best advice for any cataloguer, however new or long in the tooth, is to be aware not only of the rules we follow but the reasons they are useful for library administration, and, most importantly, for users.

It is human nature to get used to doing things the way that we do them, and in cataloguing this can sometimes lead people to find that their enjoyment of applying what RDA frequently refers to as 'cataloguer judgement' decreases. If you do nothing else to prepare for the rule change, get into the habit of choosing the books on the cataloguing shelf that will really challenge you and make you think about what you are doing and why.

As William Denton pointed out, cataloguing has been built on a set of axioms – core principles that run through all of the different rules and codes we have applied since the 19th century.

Follow what is happening on the MARC website – www.loc.gov/marc/ – even if you don't work in a MARC library. MARC is the dominant data exchange format in the library environment, and is set to remain so for the short to medium term. If you follow MARC, you will see the main elements of RDA being introduced into the library systems mainstream. They are being introduced already.

Key activities for the beginning cataloguer

The first piece of advice for beginning cataloguers should be the same as for new art historians – 'Say what you see.' Whether you are cataloguing in AACR2 or RDA, whether you are using MARC or some other in-house system, good cataloguing begins by recognizing the key features of the publication in your hands. The next stage is interpreting those features. Lastly, we describe those features according to the cataloguing rules we are following.

Think about the rules, but think also about the users of your data. How are they likely to search for the publication in your hand? What can you do, within the cataloguing standard you are using and any in-house practices, to render the publication easier to discover?

If you are new to cataloguing, don't worry about the changes. As we have indicated in this book, cataloguing rules have changed throughout the centuries, and users are still, for the most part, able to find what they are looking for in our hybrid library environment.

Each of the chapters in this book is designed to give you the core principles and the practical knowledge to begin to catalogue. We have covered AACR2 and MARC 21 in some depth because they are the leading standard and format of the day. We have covered printed books in more depth than other formats because AACR2 makes distinctions of format first, and because books, being text-based, are easier to describe in text. From the foundations of cataloguing printed books in AACR2 in MARC format, you should be able to progress to other formats.

We have discussed the new standard RDA in as much depth as is practical at a time when the only libraries that have catalogued using RDA are the US national test centres, and before the report from the test has been published. In each year since 2009 there has been an increase in the amount of time we spend on RDA in class on the MA LIS – from one hour in 2009 to four in 2011. If RDA is adopted by the majority of libraries, there will come a time when we spend more time in practicals on RDA than on other codes (including AACR2). Just so with cataloguing text books.

We hope that at the very least this book leaves you with more confidence in your knowledge than that described in Sanchez's survey in 2010.

9

The birth of RDA and the death of MARC?

One of the challenges of writing this book has been incorporating the many changes that have occurred since we began work on it in 2008. It has been hard to establish when precisely might be the right moment to bring this book into the light. When exactly would we have enough information to know what an RDA record would really look like?

Arguably, the right time would be once RDA has been implemented in a substantial number of libraries. What do we mean by 'a substantial number'? Well, certainly more than the three libraries that at time of writing (Autumn 2011) have declared they adopted RDA in order to participate in the US National Tests, and will continue to use RDA, even ahead of the Library of Congress's own adoption of the standard.

However, by the time that RDA becomes widespread, we could expect that a book like this one will not be needed. There is a genuine interest, across the cataloguing community, in how our practices and workflows *might* change. So we have written a book that reports on change and speculates on what will happen next.

Since completing the first full draft of the book, the US National Tests have reported. This chapter summarizes the recommendations contained in the test reports and in the related review of the MARC standard that the Library of Congress announced in mid-2011.

Testing resource description and access: final recommendations

The US national libraries carried out tests on RDA throughout 2011. The Library of Congress, National Agricultural Library and National Library of

Medicine were the three lead testers, but an open call was made for volunteers throughout the USA, from which 23 institutions were selected to join the three national libraries, including OCLC Metadata and Contract Services, the University of Chicago, Stanford University, Columbia University, the Music Library Association/OLAC and Backstage Library Works. A full list of testers is provided on page 31 of the final test report (US RDA Test Coordinating Committee, 2011). There were also a large number of 'informal testers' – institutions that contributed data for analysis by the Test Coordinating Committee.

Building on a methodology developed when the CONSER Standard Record was adopted, the Test Coordinating Committee devised a set of 25 materials, which every institution catalogued twice (the Common Original Set), and five records created using copy cataloguing methods (the Common Copy Set). Beyond that, libraries followed their existing workflows and procedures as far as possible, while contributing a range of further records.

The Common Original Set was used to make a comparison of the time taken between using current cataloguing rules (most often AACR2, but other standards were used if they were in normal use in the test institution) and using RDA. The records for these materials also provided an opportunity to consider the usability of the new standard and the overall consistency of the record produced (whether or not all the institutions interpreted the RDA rules in the same way).

Each test institution was also asked to create at least 25 original RDA records for items encountered in the course of its usual workflows (the Extra Original Set) and institutions also had the option of submitting edited records undertaken in copy cataloguing (the Extra Copy Set).

Cataloguers were asked to complete a survey for each record they created. There were also surveys to gather demographic information about the record creators, including information on their training (the Record Creator Profile Survey), to understand the records' ease of use and comprehension (the Record User Survey) and to capture management information on the impact of RDA implementation (the Institutional Questionnaire).

These records plus those submitted by the informal testers provided the Test Coordinating Committee with far more records and accompanying surveys than they had expected: 1,200 for the Common Original Set; 5,908 for the Extra Original Set; 111 for the Common Copy Set; and 801 for the Extra Copy Set.

The Test Coordinating Committee also received 80 responses to a questionnaire designed for the informal testers.

The full results and data analysis are presented in the *Report and Recommendations* (Library of Congress Network Developmnent and MARC Standards Office, 2010; US RDA Test Coordinating Committee, 2011), which includes helpful graphs and pie charts, and appendices including the survey questions and a breakdown of lessons learned that could be applicable for any future testing of cataloguing standards. There is much in this 184-page document that is of interest.

With regard to *practical* cataloguing, the recommendations are of most immediate relevance. Overall the test found that RDA's own goals were only partially met, and there were grave concerns about the language used in the cataloguing code – it was found to be difficult to understand and, possibly a worse indictment for a cataloguing standard, in places the language was found to be ambiguous, or capable of differing interpretations.

The Test Coordinating Committee recommended that 'RDA should be implemented by LC [the Library of Congress], NAL [the National Agricultural Library], and NLM [the National Library of Medicine] no sooner than January 2013". So it is fair to say that RDA will be the future of cataloguing, but not within the next 12 months.

Further, the report recommended: 'The three national libraries should commit resources to ensure progress is made on these activities that will require significant effort from many in and beyond the library community.' So libraries (in the USA, at least) should not feel they will be alone when the time comes to implement RDA. Outside the USA, the cataloguing community is already benefiting from the training materials published on the Library of Congress website, and expertise developed by testers such as Stanford University and University of Chicago is already being shared through presentations and articles.

The cataloguing community expressed relief at the recommendation that the JSC should 'rewrite the RDA instructions in clear, unambiguous, plain English'. In particular, the following chapters were highlighted as being priorities for rewording:

- RDA 2 Recording Attributes of Manifestation and Item
- RDA 6 Identifying Works and Expressions

- RDA 9 Identifying Persons
- RDA 10 Identifying Families
- RDA 11 Identifying Corporate Bodies
- RDA 17 General Guidelines on Recording Primary Relationships.

Another popular recommendation is that ALA Publishing should 'improve the functionality of the RDA Toolkit'. Further usability testing was also recommended. ALA Publishing was also asked to 'develop full RDA record examples in MARC and other encoding schemas... Include examples for special communities (e.g. serials, rare books, music)'.

The other recommendations, as expressed in the executive summary, were to:

- define process for updating RDA in the online environment
- announce completion of the registered RDA element sets and vocabularies
- ensure and facilitate community involvement
- lead and co-ordinate RDA training
- solicit demonstrations of prototype input and discovery systems that use the RDA element set (including relationships).

Each of the recommendations has a timeframe against it, which you can see in the full document and the executive summary.

Arguably the recommendation that brought the most joy to some parts of the cataloguing community and the most shock to others was the recommendation that within the next 18–24 months (from June 2011), they should 'Demonstrate credible progress towards a replacement for MARC'.

'MARC must die'

Attendees of CILIP's Executive Briefing on RDA 2011 in Manchester were moved to hear Beacher Wiggins announce that, having begun his career working on the implementation of the MARC format, he was about to be involved in its replacement.

As Appendix M of the Test Coordinating Committee's final report, the Library of Congress included *Transforming our Bibliographic Framework: a statement from the Library of Congress.* The document was also issued as a press release, and quickly swept through the cataloguing and general library press. As the statement put it:

> The Library of Congress has invested considerable resources in the development of broadly implemented encoding standards such as MARC 21 … Spontaneous comments from participants in the US RDA Test show that a broad cross-section of the community feels budgetary pressures but nevertheless considers it necessary to replace MARC 21 in order to reap the full benefit of new and emerging content standards.

In order to investigate the use of its resources for data exchange, the Library of Congress will:

- determine which aspects of current metadata encoding standards should be retained and evolved into a format for the future
- experiment with the semantic web and linked data technologies to see what benefits to the bibliographic framework they offer our community
- foster maximum re-use of library metadata in the broader web search environment
- enable users to navigate relationships among entities – such as persons, places, organizations, and concepts – to search more precisely in library catalogues and in the broader internet
- explore approaches to displaying metadata beyond current MARC-based systems
- identify the risks of action and inaction, including an assessment of the pace of change acceptable to the broader community
- plan to bring existing metadata into new bibliographic systems within the broader Library of Congress technical infrastructure.

For some time there has been a gradual rise of articles criticizing MARC for the very attribute that made it so useful in the early days of data exchange – its rigidity. In modern systems, the need to hold records securely in a threatening environment has been superseded by the demands to provide flexible records through linked data. In the months leading up to the Library of Congress's announcement, there was a rise in the use of the twitter hashtag

#marcmustdie as it became clear that in presenting RDA within MARC some of the new code's flexibility was being lost.

So, as this book goes to press, this is where we stand: at the dawn of a new era in cataloguing, heralded by a new cataloguing code, RDA, which is still a year away for most of us. As a result of the US National Tests, those of us who download data from consortia have encountered RDA records, and with three of the test institutions continuing to catalogue in RDA, even those of us who do not create records in the new standard need to be able to edit it within our copy cataloguing.

In short, the catalogue is hybrid, and, arguably, we are more aware of its hybrid nature than we have ever been. As we step into the future, we rely on our general cataloguing principles and our understanding of our users' needs to carry us through.

10

Examples

RDA does not have a particular format in which it prefers to be expressed. For ease of comparison, RDA records here are structured in the card format set out in AACR2.

Sample records for J.H. Bowman. *Essential cataloguing*. London: Facet Publishing, 2007.

AACR2 level 1

Bowman, J.H.

Essential cataloguing. – Repr. with corrections. – Facet, 2007. – viii, 216 p. – Previous ed.: 2003. – 9781856044561

Essential cataloguing

J. H. Bowman

facet publishing

Figure 10.1 *Title page of Essential cataloguing, by J.H. Bowman*

AACR2 level 2

Bowman, J.H.

Essential cataloguing / J.H. Bowman. – Repr. with corrections. – London : Facet, 2007. – viii, 216 p. : ill., facsims. ; 25 cm. – Previous ed.: 2003. – 9781856044561

© J. H. Bowman 2003

Published by
Facet Publishing
7 Ridgmount Street
London WC1E 7AE

Facet Publishing is wholly owned by CILIP: the Chartered Institute of Library and Information Professionals.

Except as otherwise permitted under the Copyright Designs and Patents Act 1988 this publication may only be reproduced, stored or transmitted in any form or by any means, with the prior permission of the publisher, or, in the case of reprographic reproduction, in accordance with the terms of a licence issued by The Copyright Licensing Agency. Enquiries concerning reproduction outside those terms should be sent to Facet Publishing, 7 Ridgmount Street, London WC1E 7AE.

First published 2003
Reprinted 2003, 2004, 2005, 2006, 2007 (with corrections), 2008

British Library Cataloguing in Publication Data
A catalogue record for this book is available from the British Library.

ISBN 978-1-85604-456-1

Typeset in Plantin and Gill Sans by Facet Publishing.
Printed and made in Great Britain by MPG Books Ltd, Bodmin, Cornwall.

Figure 10.2 *Title page verso of Essential cataloguing, by J.H. Bowman*

RDA

Essential cataloguing / J.H. Bowman. – Reprinted with corrections. – London : Facet Publishing, 2007. – viii, 216 pages : illustrations, facsimiles ; 25 cm. – Previous edition: 2003. – 9781856044561
Access point: Bowman, J.H.

MARC 21 (AACR2)

020		$a9781856044561 (pbk)
100	1	$aBowman, J.H.
245	10	$aEssential cataloguing /
		$cJ.H. Bowman
250		$aRepr. with corrections
260		$aLondon :
		$bFacet,
		$c2007
300		$aviii, 216 p. :
		$bill., facsims. ;
		$c25 cm.
500		$aPrevious ed.: 2003.

Sample records for Derek Adams. *Unconcerned but not indifferent*. Colchester: Ninth Arrondissement, 2006.

AACR2 level 1

Adams, Derek

Unconcerned but not indifferent. – Ninth Arrondissement, 2006. – 32 p. – 9780955352119

Figure 10.3 *Cover page of Unconcerned but not indifferent, by Derek Adams*

AACR2 level 2

Adams, Derek

Unconcerned but not indifferent : the life of Man Ray / Derek Adams. –
Colchester : Ninth Arrondissement, 2006. – 32 p. ; 21 cm. – 9780955352119

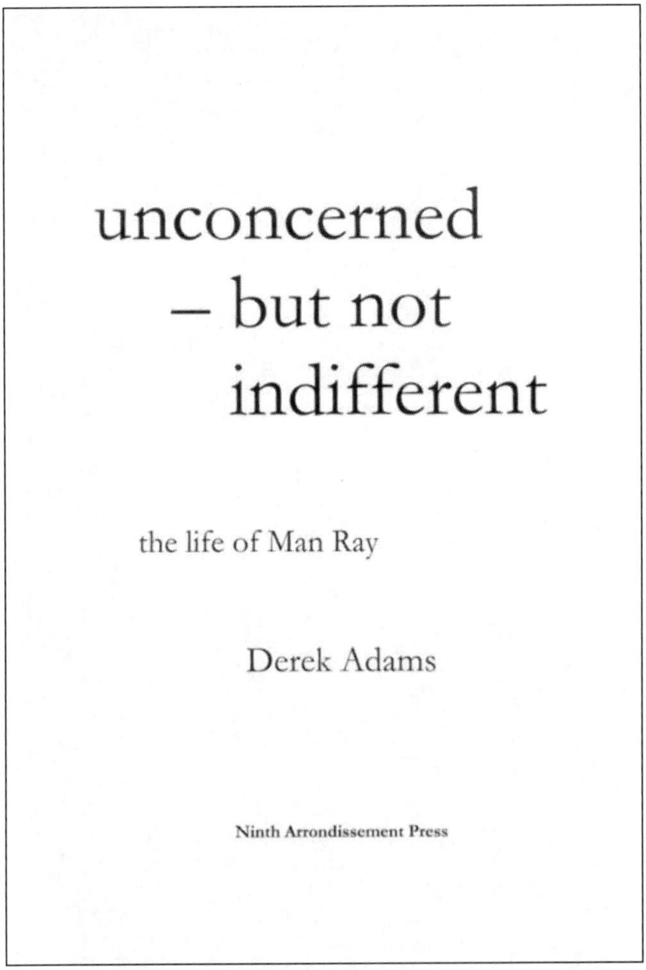

unconcerned
– but not
indifferent

the life of Man Ray

Derek Adams

Ninth Arrondissement Press

Figure 10.4 *Title page of Unconcerned but not indifferent, by Derek Adams*

RDA

Unconcerned – but not indifferent : the life of Man Ray / Derek Adams. –
Colchester : Ninth Arrondissement Press, 2006. – 32 pages ; 21 cm. –
9780955352119
Access point: Adams, Derek

For Michael Donaghy, who is missed by everyone.

Acknowledgements
I would like to thank the editors of the following magazines, where
some of these poems first appeared: Comrades, Chimera, Nthposition,
Magma, SpinDrifter, Stride.
Grateful thanks to Kathryn Maris & the Morley group, the Adamatines
and the long suffering Arvonauts for support and comments.
Robert Cole & Susie Reynolds for their excitement about this project
and encouragement to see it through.
And finally Dolly for putting up with having poems thrust before her to
look at whilst trying to finish her degree thesis.

Poems copyright Derek Adams 2006

Also by Derek Adams
Postcards to Olympus
Everday Objects, Chance Remarks

Published 2006
Ninth Arrondissement Press
118 Nayland Road,
Mile End,
Colchester CO4 5ET.

ISBN 978 0 9553521 1 9

2

Figure 10.5 *Title page verso of Unconcerned but not indifferent, by Derek Adams*

MARC 21 (AACR2)

020		$a9780955352119 (pbk)
100	1	$aAdams, Derek
245	10	$aUnconcerned but not indifferent :
		$bthe life of Man Ray /
		$cDerek Adams
260		$aColchester :
		$bNinth Arrondissement,
		$c2006
300		$a32 p. ;
		$c21 cm.

Sample records for Pascale Petit. *The wounded deer*. Huddersfield: Smith Doorstop, 2005.

AACR2 level 1

Petit, Pascale, 1953-

The wounded deer. – Smith/Doorstop, 2005. – 24 p. – 1902382757

Figure 10.6 *Detachable cover of The wounded deer, by Pascale Petit*

AACR2 level 2

Petit, Pascale, 1953-

The wounded deer : [fourteen poems after Frida Kahlo] / Pascale Petit. –
Huddersfield : Smith/Doorstop, 2005. – 24 p. ; 19 cm. – Other title information
from half-title page. –1902382757

The Wounded Deer

Pascale Petit

Smith/Doorstop Books

Figure 10.7 *Title page of The wounded deer, by Pascale Petit*

RDA

The wounded deer : fourteen poems after Frida Kahlo / Pascale Petit. –
Hudersfield : Smith/Doorstep Books, 2005. – 24 pages ; 19 cm. – 1902382757
Access point: Petit, Pascale, 1953-

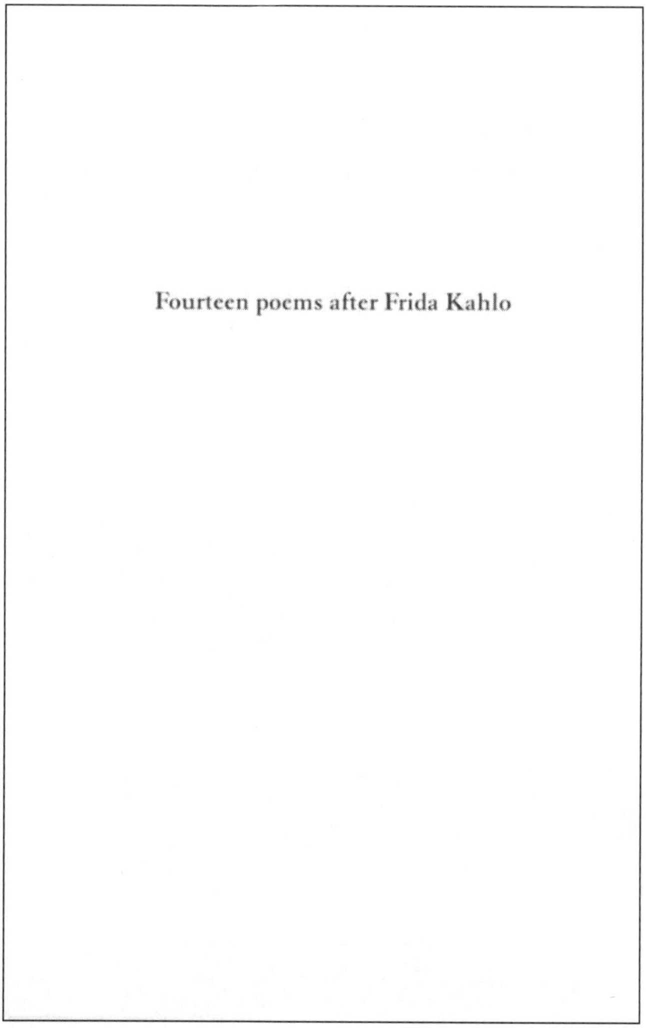

Fourteen poems after Frida Kahlo

Figure 10.8 *Half-title page of The wounded deer, by Pascale Petit*

MARC 21 (AACR2)

020		$a1902382757 (pbk)
100	1	$aPetit, Pascale,
		$d1953-
245	14	$aThe wounded deer :
		$b[fourteen poems after Frida Kahlo] /
		$cPascale Petit
260		$aHuddersfield :
		$bSmith/Doorstep,
		$c2005
300		$a24 p. ;
		$c19 cm.
500		$aOther title information from half-title page.

Published 2005 by
Smith/Doorstop Books
The Poetry Business
The Studio
Byram Arcade
Westgate
Huddersfield HD1 1ND

Copyright © Pascale Petit 2005
All Rights Reserved

ISBN 1-902382-75-7
Printed by Swiftprint, Huddersfield

The Poetry Business gratefully acknowledges the help of Arts
Council England and Kirklees Metropolitan Council.

Acknowledgements
Many thanks to the editors of the following, in which some
of these poems first appeared: *American Poetry Review*,
Antologia Letras en el Golfo (Mexico), *The Canary*, *Free Verse*,
The Gift, *Kenyon Review*, *Magma*, *Mslexia*, *Poetry Wales*, *The
Pterodactyl's Wing*, *Quadrant* (Australia), and *Tabla*.
The author is very grateful to the Royal Literary Fund for
financial support to finish this pamphlet.

Previous publications:
Icefall Climbing (Smith/Doorstop 1994)
Heart of a Deer (Enitharmon 1998)
Tying the Song (Enitharmon 2000) (co-edited with Mimi
Khalvati)
The Zoo Father (Seren 2001)
The Huntress (Seren 2005)

Figure 10.9 *Half-title page verso of The wounded deer, by Pascale Petit*

Sample records for Jasmine Ann Cooray. *Everything we don't say*. London: Tall Lighthouse, 2009.
AACR2 level 1

Cooray, Jasmine Ann
Everything we don't say. – Tall-Lighthouse, 2009. – 13 p. – 9781904551607

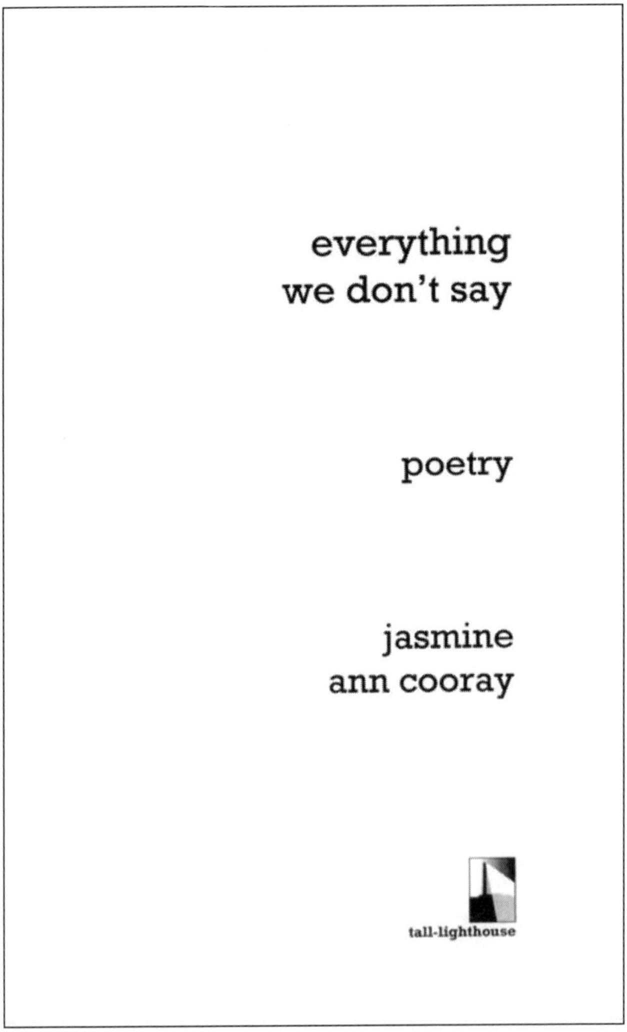

everything
we don't say

poetry

jasmine
ann cooray

tall-lighthouse

Figure 10.10 *Title page of Everything we don't say, by Jasmine Ann Cooray*

AACR2 level 2

Cooray, Jasmine Ann

Everything we don't say : poetry / Jasmine Ann Cooray. – [London] : Tall-Lighthouse, 2009. – 13 p. ; 21 cm. – 9781904551607

For my family, where resilience meets laughter.

Acknowledgements and thanks are due to the editors and publishers of **Flight Pt. 1** where some of these poems, or versions of them first appeared.

There have been a lot of rungs and leg ups, so I'll just say this; thank you to my families; biological, poetical, emotional and all else in-between- those who kick backsides, who tickle bellies, who stroke foreheads. I have courage because of you. I smile because of you.

The epigraph is from the poem Discovering Fire, by Ellen Bass in the collection *The Human Line* (Copper Canyon Press, Washington 2007)

cover image: detail from sculpture by
          sally renwick (www.sallyrenwick.com)

cover photo: kevin davis (www.imagecounterpoint.com)

© Jasmine Ann Cooray 2009
Jasmine Ann Cooray has asserted her rights
under the Copyright, Design & Patents Act 1988
to be identified as the author of this work.

published 2009
ISBN 978 1 904551 60 7
www.tall-lighthouse.co.uk

Figure 10.11 *Title page verso of Everything we don't say, by Jasmine Ann Cooray*

RDA

Everything we don't say : poetry / Jasmine Ann Cooray. – [London] : tall-lighthouse, 2009. – 13 pages ; 21 cm. – 9781904551607
Access point: Cooray, Jasmine Ann

MARC 21 (AACR2)

020		$a9781904551607 (pbk)
100	1	$aCooray, Jasmine Ann
245	10	$aEverything we don't say :
		$bpoetry /
		$cJasmine Ann Cooray
260		$a[London] :
		$bTall-Lighthouse,
		$c2009
300		$a13 p. ;
300		$c21 cm.

Sample records for Joanna Ezekiel. *Centuries of skin*. Snitterfield: Ragged Raven, 2010.

AACR2 level 1

Ezekiel, Joanna, 1969-

Centuries of skin. – Ragged Raven, 2010. – 79 p. – 9780955255298

Joanna Ezekiel

CENTURIES OF SKIN

Ragged Raven Press

3

Figure 10.12 *Title page of Centuries of skin, by Joanna Ezekiel*

AACR2 level 2

Ezekiel, Joanna, 1969-

Centuries of skin / Joanna Ezekiel. – Snitterfield, Warwickshire : Ragged Raven, 2010. – 79 p. ; 21 cm. – 9780955255298

CENTURIES OF SKIN

First published in England, 2010 by Ragged Raven Press
I Lodge Farm, Snitterfield, Warwickshire CV37 0LR
email: raggedravenpress@aol.com

website: www.raggedraven.co.uk

© Joanna Ezekiel, 2010

The moral rights of the author are asserted in accordance with the
Copyright, Designs and Patent Act, 1988

Centuries of skin
ISBN 978 0 9552552 9 8

All rights reserved. No part of this book may be reproduced, stored
in a database or other retrieval system, or transmitted in any form,
by any means, including mechanical, electronic, photocopying,
recording or otherwise, without the prior written permission of the
publisher, except activities by the poet, or for the purpose of critical
review, personal study or non-profit-making discussion.

Set in Arial.

Printed by Short Run Press Limited, Exeter, England.

2

Figure 10.13 *Facing the title page of Centuries of skin, by Joanna Ezekiel*

RDA

Centuries of skin / Joanna Ezekiel. – Snitterfield, Warwickshire : Ragged Raven Press, 2010. – 79 pages ; 21 cm. – 9780955255298

Access point: Ezekiel, Joanna, 1969-

MARC 21 (AACR2)

020		$a9780955255298 (pbk)
100	1	$aEzekiel, Joanna,
		$d1969-
245	10	$aCenturies of skin /
		$cJoanna Ezekiel
260		$aSnitterfield, Warwickshire :
		$bRagged Raven,
		$c2010
300		$a79 p. ;
300		$c21 cm.

Sample records for Henry Charles Moore. *Noble deeds of the world's heroines*. London: Religious Tract Society, 1903.

AACR2 level 1

Moore, Henry Charles

Noble deeds of the world's heroines. – Religious Tract Society, [1903]. – 286 p., [15] leaves of plates. – Publication date from British Library catalogue.

Added entry: Religious Tract Society

Noble Deeds of the World's Heroines

By

HENRY CHARLES MOORE

WITH FIFTEEN PAGE ILLUSTRATIONS

London
The Religious Tract Society
56 Paternoster Row and 65 St. Paul's Churchyard

Figure 10.14 *Title page of Noble deeds of the world's heroines, by Henry Charles Moore*

AACR2 level 2

Moore, Henry Charles
Noble deeds of the world's heroines / by Henry Charles Moore. – London :
Religious Tract Society, [1903]. – 286 p., [15] leaves of plates : ill. ; 21 cm. –
(Brave deeds series). – Publication date from British Library catalogue.\
Added entry: Religious Tract Society

RDA

Noble deeds of the world's heroines / by Henry Charles Moore. – London :
Religious Tract Society, [1903]. – 286 p., [15] leaves of plates : illustrations ; 21
cm. – (Brave deeds series). – Publication date from British Library catalogue.
Access point: Religious Tract Society

MARC 21 (AACR2)

100	1	$aMoore, Henry Charles
245	10	$aNoble deeds of the world's heroines /
		$cby Henry Charles Moore.
260		$aLondon :
		$bReligious Tract Society,
		$c[1903]
300		$a286 p., [15] leaves of plates :
		$bill. ;
300		$c21 cm.
490	1	$aBrave deeds series
500		$aPublication date from British Library catalogue.
710	1	$aReligious Tract Society
830	0	$aBrave deeds series

Sample records for W. Carew Hazlitt (ed.). *The essays of Michel de Montaigne*. London: George Bell & Sons, 1892.

AACR2 level 1

Montaigne, Michel de, 1533-1592

The essays of Michel de Montaigne. Vol. II / translated by Charles Cotton ; edited with some account of the life of the author, and notes, by W. Carew Hazlitt. – 2nd ed., rev. – George Bell & Sons, 1892. – 522 p.

Added entry: Cotton, Charles, 1630-1687

Added entry: Hazlitt, William Carew, 1834-1913

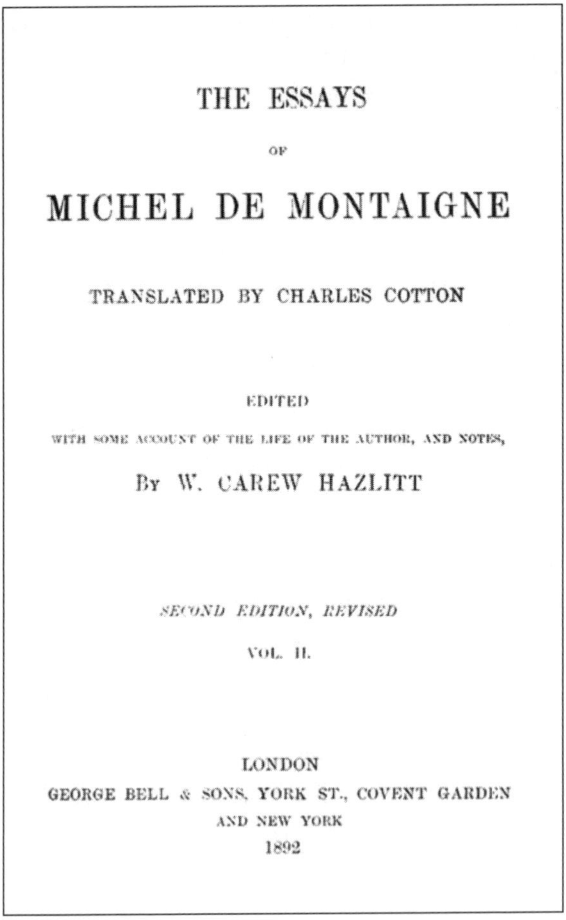

THE ESSAYS

OF

MICHEL DE MONTAIGNE

TRANSLATED BY CHARLES COTTON

EDITED

WITH SOME ACCOUNT OF THE LIFE OF THE AUTHOR, AND NOTES,

BY W. CAREW HAZLITT

SECOND EDITION, REVISED

VOL. II.

LONDON
GEORGE BELL & SONS, YORK ST., COVENT GARDEN
AND NEW YORK
1892

Figure 10.15 *Title page of The essays of Michel de Montaigne, edited by W. Carew Hazlitt*

AACR2 level 2

Montaigne, Michel de, 1533-1592

The essays of Michel de Montaigne. Vol. II / translated by Charles Cotton ;
edited with some account of the life of the author, and notes, by W. Carew
Hazlitt. – 2nd ed., rev. – London : George Bell & Sons, 1892. – 522 p. ; 19 cm. –
(Bohn's Standard Library).
Added entry: Cotton, Charles, 1630-1687
Added entry: Hazlitt, William Carew, 1834-1913

CHISWICK PRESS:—C. WHITTINGHAM AND CO., TOOKS COURT,
CHANCERY LANE.

Figure 10.16 *Title page verso of The essays of Michel de Montaigne, edited by W. Carew
Hazlitt*

RDA

The essays of Michel de Montaigne. Vol. II / translated by Charles Cotton ;
edited with some account of the life of the author, and notes, by W. Carew
Hazlitt. – Second edition, revised. – London : George Bell & Sons, 1892. – 522
pages ; 19 cm. – (Bohn's Standard Library).
Access point: Montaigne, Michel de, 1533-1592
Access point: Cotton, Charles, 1630-1687, translator
Access point: Hazlitt, William Carew, 1834-1913, editor

MARC 21 (AACR2)

100	1	$aMontaigne, Michel de, $d1533-1592
245	14	$aThe essays of Michel de Montaigne. Vol. II / $ctranslated by Charles Cotton ; edited with some account of the life of the author, and notes, by W. Carew Hazlitt
250		$a2nd ed., rev.
260		$aLondon : $bGeorge Bell & Sons, $c1892
300		$a522 p. ;
300		$c19 cm.
490	1	$aBohn's Standard Library
700	1	$aCotton, Charles, $d1630-1687
830	0	$aBohn's Standard Library

Sample records for David Pearson. *Provenance research in book history: a handbook*. London: British Library, 1998.

AACR2 level 1

Pearson, David, 1955-

Provenance research in book history. – Repr. with a new introduction. – British Library, 1998. – xiv, 326 p. – Previous ed.: 1994. Includes bibliographies and index. – 0712345981

Added entry: British Library

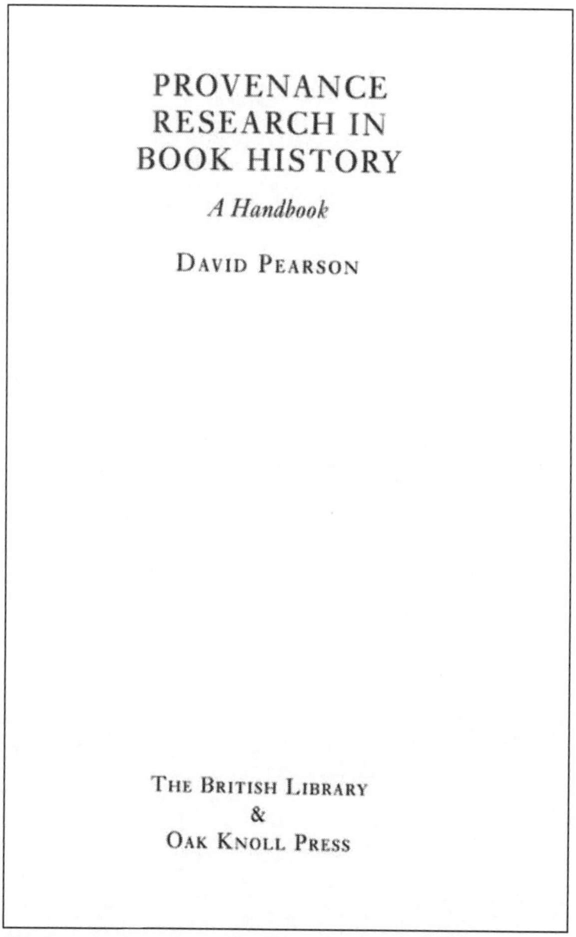

PROVENANCE
RESEARCH IN
BOOK HISTORY

A Handbook

DAVID PEARSON

THE BRITISH LIBRARY
&
OAK KNOLL PRESS

Figure 10.17 *Title page of Provenance research in book history: a handbook, by David Pearson*

AACR2 level 2

Pearson, David, 1955-

Provenance research in book history : a handbook / David Pearson. – Repr. with a new introduction. – London : British Library ; New Castle : Oak Knoll, 1998. – xiv, 326 p. : ill., facsims. ; 23 cm. – (British Library Studies in the History of the Book). – Previous ed.: 1994. – Includes bibliographies and index. – 0712345981

Added entry: British Library

For my parents,
with thanks for the earliest bibliographical encouragement

First published 1994 by The British Library
Reprinted with a new Introduction 1998
by The British Library
96 Euston Road
London NW1 2DB
UK

Marketed exclusively in North and South America, including Canada
by Oak Knoll Press
308 Delaware Street
New Castle
DE 19720
USA

© 1994, 1998 David Pearson

ISBN 0 7123 0344 8 (BL cased edition)
ISBN 0 7123 4598 1 (BL paperback edition)
ISBN 1 884718 79 5 (Oak Knoll cased edition)
ISBN 1 884718 80 9 (Oak Knoll paperback edition)

Designed by John Trevitt
Typeset by Norman Tilley Graphics, Northampton
Printed in England by Henry Ling, Dorchester

Figure 10.18 *Title page verso of Provenance research in book history: a handbook, by David Pearson*

RDA

Provenance research in book history : a handbook / David Pearson. – Reprinted
with a new introduction. – London : British Library ; New Castle : Oak Knoll
Press, 1998. – xiv, 326 pages : illustrations, facsimiles ; 23 cm. – (British Library
Studies in the History of the Book). – Previous edition: 1994. – Includes
bibliographies and index. – 0712345981
Access point: Pearson, David, 1955-
Access point: British Library

MARC 21 (AACR2)

020		$a0712345981 (pbk)
100	1	$aPearson, David,
		$d1955-
245	14	$aProvenance research in book history :
		$ba handbook /
		$cDavid Pearson
250		$aRepr. with a new introduction
260		$aLondon :
		$bBritish Library ;
		$aNew Castle :
		$bOak Knoll,
		$c1998
300		$axiv, 326p. :
		$bill., facsims. ;
		$c23 cm.
490	1	$aBritish Library Studies in the History of the Book
710	1	$aBritish Library
830	0	$aBritish Library Studies in the History of the Book

Sample records for John H. Ingram (ed.). *The poetical works of Elizabeth Barrett Browning, from 1862 to 1844*. London: Griffith, Farran, Okeden & Welsh, [18--].

AACR2 level 1

Browning, Elizabeth Barrett, 1806-1861

The poetical works of Elizabeth Barrett Browning, from 1826 to 1844 / edited, with a memoir, by John H. Ingram. – Griffith, Farran, Okedin & Welsh, [18--]. – xvi, 400 p.

Added entry: Ingram, John Henry, 1842-1916

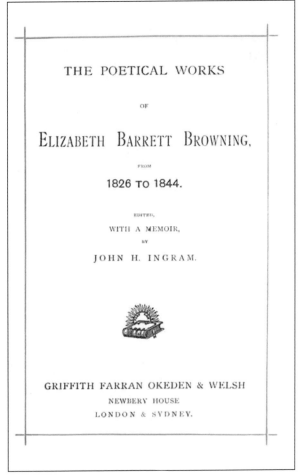

THE POETICAL WORKS

OF

ELIZABETH BARRETT BROWNING,

FROM

1826 TO 1844.

EDITED,

WITH A MEMOIR,

BY

JOHN H. INGRAM.

GRIFFITH FARRAN OKEDEN & WELSH
NEWBERY HOUSE
LONDON & SYDNEY.

Figure 10.19 *Title page of The poetical works of Elizabeth Barrett Browning, from 1862 to 1844, edited by John H. Ingram*

AACR2 level 2

Browning, Elizabeth Barrett, 1806-1861
[Poems. Selections] The poetical works of Elizabeth Barrett Browning, from 1826 to 1844 / edited, with a memoir, by John H. Ingram. – London ; Sydney : Griffith, Farran, Okedin & Welsh, [18--]. – xvi, 400 p. : frontis., port. ; 19 cm.
Added entry: Ingram, John Henry, 1842-1916

RDA

The poetical works of Elizabeth Barrett Browning, from 1826 to 1844 / edited, with a memoir, by John H. Ingram. – London ; Sydney : Griffith, Farran, Okedin & Welsh, [1880s?]. – xvi, 400 pages : frontispiece, portrait ; 19 cm.
Access point: Browning, Elizabeth Barrett, 1806-1861
Access point: Ingram, John Henry, 1842-1916, editor

MARC 21 (AACR2)

100	**1**	$a Browning, Elizabeth Barrett, $d1806-1861
240	**10**	$aPoems. Selections
245	**14**	$aThe poetical works of Elizabeth Barrett Browning, from 1826 to 1844 / $cedited, with a memoir, by John H. Ingram
260		$aLondon ; $bSydney : $aGriffith, Farran, Okedin & Welsh, $c[18--]
300		$axvi, 400 p. : $bfacsim., port. ; $c19 cm.
710	**1**	$aIngram, John Henry, 1842-1916

Sample records for *The Library of Babel, in and out of place, 25 February – 13 June 2010*. London: Zabludowicz, 2010.

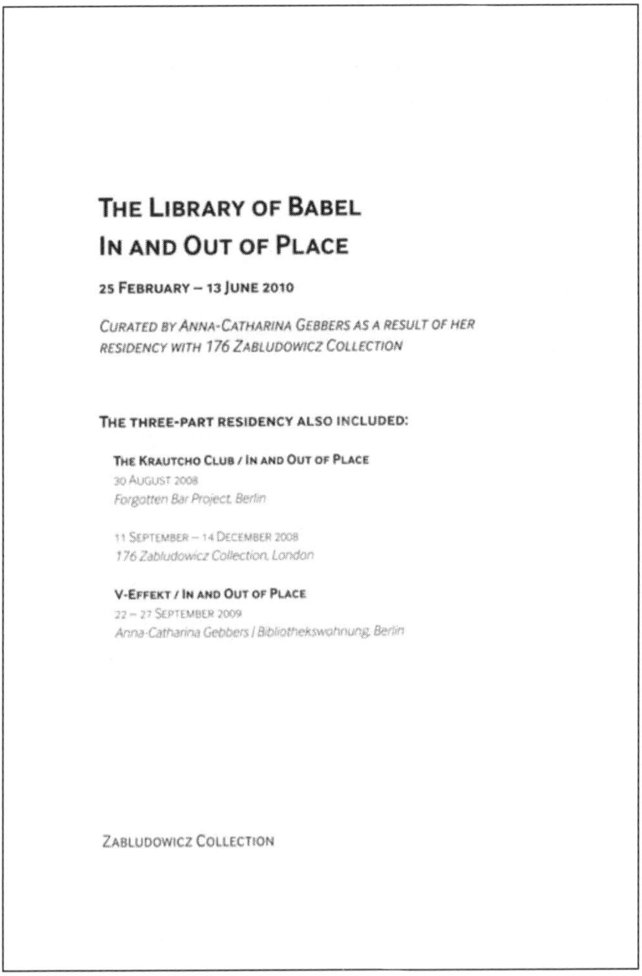

THE LIBRARY OF BABEL
IN AND OUT OF PLACE

25 FEBRUARY – 13 JUNE 2010

CURATED BY ANNA-CATHARINA GEBBERS AS A RESULT OF HER
RESIDENCY WITH 176 ZABLUDOWICZ COLLECTION

THE THREE-PART RESIDENCY ALSO INCLUDED:

THE KRAUTCHO CLUB / IN AND OUT OF PLACE
30 AUGUST 2008
Forgotten Bar Project, Berlin

11 SEPTEMBER – 14 DECEMBER 2008
176 Zabludowicz Collection, London

V-EFFEKT / IN AND OUT OF PLACE
22 – 27 SEPTEMBER 2009
Anna-Catharina Gebbers / Bibliothekswohnung, Berlin

ZABLUDOWICZ COLLECTION

Figure 10.20 *Title page of The Library of Babel, in and out of place, 25 February – 13 June 2010*

AACR2 level 1

The Library of Babel, in and out of place / curated by Anna-Catharina Gebbers as a result of her residency with 176 Zabludowicz Collection. – Zabludowicz, 2010. – 120 p. – "Edited by Ellen Mara de Wachter." -- colophon. – 9780955662980

 Added entry: Gebbers, Anna-Catharina

 Added entry: De Wachter, Ellen Mara, 1977-

 Added entry: Zabludowicz Collection

COLOPHON

**THE LIBRARY OF BABEL /
IN AND OUT OF PLACE**
Curated by Anna-Catharina Gebbers
Edited by Ellen Mara De Wachter
© The authors and Zabludowicz Art Projects, 2010
All texts are copyright of the authors
Installation photography by Thierry Bal
Designed by JOFF + OLLIE
Proofread by Chrissy Williams
Anna-Catharina Gebbers' essay translated
from the German by Jacqueline Todd
Additional photographs by:
Tim Bowditch (p. 95 – 98); David Bebber (p. 88);
Anna-Catharina Gebbers (p.92); Will Leach (p. 91)

176 Zabludowicz Collection:
Curator and Head of Collection: Elizabeth Neilson
Exhibitions Curator: Ellen Mara De Wachter
Interaction Curator: Maitreyi Maheshwari
Collection Manager: Ginie Morysse
Assistant Collection Manager: Kelly Wojtko
Front of House Manager: Bryony Hewetson
IT/Building Manager: Marc-Antoine Filippini
PA to Anita Zabludowicz: Caragh Quinlan
Intern: Amy Budd
Gallery Assistants: David Angus, Tim Bowditch,
Chloe Cooper, Matthew de Kersaint Giraudeau,
Bella Perry

Advisory Board:
Brian Boylan
Thomas Dane
James Lingwood

ISBN: 978-0-9556629-8-0

**This publication has been produced in a
limited edition of 500 to coincide with
The Library of Babel / In and Out of Place,
an exhibition presented at 176 Zabludowicz
Collection, London, between 25 February
and 13 June 2010.**

176 Zabludowicz Collection are trading names
of Zabludowicz Art Projects. Zabludowicz Art
Projects is a company limited by guarantee
(company registered number 6269591). Registered
charity number 1120067. Registered office: 41
Dover Street, London W1S 4NS

No part of this publication may be reproduced or
transmitted in any form or by any means, or stored
in any retrieval system of any nature without prior
written permission of the copyright holders, except
for permitted fair dealing under the Copyright
Designs and Patents Act 1988 or in accordance
with the terms of a licence issued by the Copyright
Licensing Agency in respect of photocopying and/
or reprographic reproduction.

The information in this publication is based on
material supplied to Zabludowicz Art Projects.
While every effort has been made to ensure its
accuracy, Zabludowicz Art Projects does not under
any circumstances accept responsibility for errors
or omissions.

A catalogue record of this publication is available
from the British Library.

176 Prince of Wales Road
London NW5 3PT
Tel +44 (0) 20 7428 8940
Fax +44 (0) 20 7428 8949
info@projectspace176.com

[120]

Figure 10.21 *Colophon of The Library of Babel, in and out of place, 25 February – 13 June 2010*

AACR2 level 2

The Library of Babel, in and out of place : 25 February – 13 June 2010 / curated by Anna-Catharina Gebbers as a result of her residency with 176 Zabludowicz Collection. – London : Zabludowicz, 2010. – 120 p. : col. ill. ; 24 cm. – "Edited by Ellen Mara de Wachter." -- colophon. - "This publication has been produced in a limited edition of 500 to coincide with The Library of Babel/In and Out of Place, an exhibition presented at 176 Zabludowicz Collection, London, between 25 February and 13 June 2010." -- colophon. – 9780955662980
Added entry: Gebbers, Anna-Catharina
Added entry: De Wachter, Ellen Mara, 1977-
Added entry: Zabludowicz Collection

RDA

The Library of Babel, in and out of place : 25 February – 13 June 2010 / curated by Anna-Catharina Gebbers as a result of her residency with 176 Zabludowicz Collection. – London : Zabludowicz Art Projects, 2010. – 120 pages : colour illustrations ; 24 cm. – "Edited by Ellen Mara de Wachter." -- colophon. - "This publication has been produced in a limited edition of 500 to coincide with The Library of Babel/In and Out of Place, an exhibition presented at 176 Zabludowicz Collection, London, between 25 February and 13 June 2010." -- colophon. – 9780955662980
Access point: Gebbers, Anna-Catharina, curator
Access point: De Wachter, Ellen Mara, 1977-, editor
Access point: Zabludowicz Collection

MARC 21 (AACR2)

020		$a9780955662980 (pbk)
245	04	$aThe Library of Babel, in and out of place:
		$b25 February – 13 June 2010 /
		$ccurated by Anna-Catharina Gebbers as a result of her residency with 176 Zabludowicz Collection
260		$aLondon :
		$bZabludowicz,
		$c2010

300		$a120 p. :
		$bcol. ill. ;
300		$c24 cm.
500		$a"Editied by Ellen Mara De Wachter." -- colophon.
500		$a"This publication has been produced in a limited edition of 500 to coincide with The Library of Babel/In and Out of Place, an exhibition presented at 176 Zabludowicz Collection, London, between 25 February and 13 June 2010" -- colophon.
700	1	$aGebbers, Anna-Catharina
700	1	$aDe Wachter, Ellen Mara,
		$d1977-
710	2	$aZabludowicz Collection

References

Bowman, J. H. (2007) *Essential Cataloguing*, repr. with corrections, Facet Publishing.

British Museum Department of Printed Books (1841) Rules for the Compilation of the Catalogue, British Museum.

Carlton, S. (2011) A Nearly New Professional, *Catalogue & Index*, **162**, 17.

Chan, L. M. (2007) *Cataloging and Classification: an introduction*, 3rd edn, Scarecrow.

Cutter, C. A. (1891) *Rules for a Dictionary Catalogue*, 3rd edn, Government Printing Office.

Danskin, A. (2010) *RDA in the UK: summary of results: [CILIP Cataloguing & Indexing Group Conference, 2010]*, www.cilip.org.uk/get-involved/special-interest-groups/cataloguing-indexing/Documents/CIG%20Conference%202010/2010DanskinA.ppt.

Denton, W. (2007) FRBR and the History of Cataloging. In Taylor, A. G. (ed.), *Understanding FRBR: what it is and how it will affect our retrieval tools*, Libraries Unlimited.

Fforde, J. (2003) *The Well of Lost Plots*, Hodder & Stoughton.

Fforde, J. (2002) *Lost in a Good Book*, Hodder & Stoughton.

Gaskell, P. (1995) *A New Introduction to Bibliography*, Oak Knoll.

Grim, G. (2011) A New Professional, *Catalogue & Index*, **162**, 15-165.

Higgs, E. (2011) Personal Identification as Information Flows in England, 1500–2000. In Weller, T. (ed.), *Information History in the Modern World: histories of the information age*, Palgrave Macmillan.

Howard, J. (2011) Learning to Catalogue in 2010–11, *Catalogue & Index*, **163**, 1011.

IFLA (1998) *Functional Requirements for Bibliographic Records: final report*, UCBIM Publications New Series 19, www.ifla.org/files/cataloguing/frbr/frbr.pdf.

IFLA (2005) *Functional Requirements for Authority Records: a conceptual model, draft*, www.cidoc-crm.org/docs/frbr_oo/frbr_docs/FRANAR-Conceptual-M-Draft-e.pdf.

IFLA (2009) *Full ISBD Examples*, preliminary edn,
   www.ifla.org/files/cataloguing/isbd/isbd-examples_2009.pdf.

IFLA Cataloguing Section and IFLA Meetings of Experts on an International
   Cataloguing Code (2009) *International Statement of Cataloguing Principles*,
   www.ifla.org/publications/statement-of-international-cataloguing-principles.

IFLA Committee on Cataloguing ISBD Review Committee Working Group (1992)
   ISBD(G): General International Standard Bibliographic Description, annotated text,
   rev. edn, Saur.

IFLA Study Group on the Functional Requirements for Bibliographic Records (2009)
   Functional Requirements for Bibliographic Records: final report, last updated February
   2009, www.ifla.org/files/cataloguing/frbr/frbr_2008.pdf.

Indiana University Variations/FRBR Project (2010) *Variations/FRBR: variations as a
   testbed for the FRBR conceptual model*, last updated 24 October 2010,
   www.dlib.indiana.edu/projects/vfrbr/.

ISNI International Agency [2011] *Sample ISNI References (for test purposes only); ISNI:
   International Standard Name Identifier, draft ISO 27729*, www.isni.org.

Joint Steering Committee for the Development of RDA 2011 (2011) *RDA: resource
   description and access, RDA Toolkit*, www.rdatoolkit.org/.

Joint Steering Committee for the Development of RDA (2010a) *RDA: Resource
   Description and Access, frequently asked questions*, www.rda-jsc.org/rdafaq.html.

Joint Steering Committee for the Development of RDA (2010b) *RDA: Resource
   Description and Access, presentations on RDA*, last updated 1 December 2010,
   www.rda-jsc.org/rdapresentations.html.

Joint Steering Committee for the Development of RDA (2008a) *RDA: Resource
   Description and Access, [Appendix] M, complete examples*, last updated 10 November
   2008, www.rdaonline.org/constituencyreview/Phase1AppM_11_10_08.pdf.

Joint Steering Committee for the Development of RDA (2008b) *Complete Examples*,
   www.rdaonline.org/constituencyreview/Phase1AppM_11_10_08.pdf.

Joint Steering Committee for Revision of AACR (2005) *Anglo-American Cataloguing
   Rules*, 2nd edn, American Library Association, Canadian Library Association and
   CILIP: the Chartered Institute of Library and Information Professionals.

Library of Congress (2003) *Library of Congress Catalog Record [for] The Organization of
   Information/Arlene G. Taylor*, 2nd edn, http://lccn.loc.gov/2003058904.

Library of Congress, National Agricultural Library and National Library of
   Medicine (2011) *Response of the Library of Congress, the National Agricultural
   Library, and the National Library of Medicine to the RDA Test Coordinating Committee,*

13 June, www.loc.gov/bibliographic-future/rda/source/rda-execstatement-13june11.pdf.

Library of Congress Cataloging and Acquisitions (2011) *Library of Congress Documentation for the RDA (Resource Description and Access) Test: RDA Test record downloads*, www.loc.gov/catdir/cpso/RDAtest/rdatest.html.

Library of Congress Network Development and MARC Standards Office (2003) *Displays for Multiple Versions from MARC 21 and FRBR*, www.loc.gov/marc/marc-functional-analysis/multiple-versions.html.

Library of Congress Network Development and MARC Standards Office (2009) *MARC 21 Authority: introduction*, last updated October 2009, www.loc.gov/marc/authority/adintro.html.

Library of Congress Network Development and MARC Standards Office (2010) *MARC 21 Format for Bibliographic Data*, last updated 21 September 2010, www.loc.gov/marc/bibliographic/.

Library of Congress Network Development and MARC Standards Office Bibliographic Framework Transition Initiative (2011) *Transforming our Bibliographic Framework: a statement from the Library of Congress (May 13, 2011)*, www.loc.gov/marc/transition/news/framework-051311.html.

Library of Congress Network Development and MARC Standards Office and Society of American Archivists (2011) *EAD: Encoded Archival Description 2002 Version Official Site*, www.loc.gov/ead/.

Little Brown (2008) *[Web page for] I (heart) my zimmer/Bill Fallover*, last updated 11 June 2008, www.littlebrown.co.uk/Title/9781847442567.

Lubetzky, S. (1946) *Studies of Descriptive Cataloging: a report to the Librarian of Congress by the Director of the Processing Department*, Washington, Government Printing Office.

Lubetzky, S. (1953) *Cataloging Rules and Principles: a critique of the ALA Rules for Entry and a proposed design for their revision*, Library of Congress.

Lubetsky, S. (1960) *Code of Cataloguing Rules, Author and Title Entry: an unfinished draft for a new edition of Cataloging Rules prepared for the Catalog Code Revision Committee, with an explanatory commentary by Paul Dunkin*, American Library Association.

Lubetsky, S. (1969) *Principles of Cataloging: final report. Phase 1: Descriptive Cataloging*, University of California Institute of Library Research.

Lubetsky, S. and Svenonius, E. (2001) The Vicissitudes of Ideology and Technology in Anglo-American Cataloguing since Panizzi and a Prospective Reformation of the Catalog for the Next Century. In Svenonius, E. and McGarry, D. (eds), *Seymour Lubetzky: writings on the classical art of cataloging*, Libraries Unlimited.

Madden, M. (2008) *Digital Footprints: identity, search, social networking*, Pew Internet and American Life Project, www.pewinternet.org/Presentations/2008/Digital-Footprints.aspx.

MARC 21: Library of Congress Network Development and MARC Standards Office (2010) *MARC 21 Format for Bibliographic Data*, last updated 21 September 2010, www.loc.gov/marc/bibliographic/.

Maule, S. (2011) Cataloguing: a view from a new professional, *Catalogue & Index*, **162**, 13.

Maxwell, R. L. (2010) *RDA in Depth: differences between RDA and AACR2: [presentation to] Utah Library Association*, 14 May, www.rda-jsc.org/docs/RDA_part_2_201005.pdf.

Meehan, T. ([2010]) *FRBR Example: The English Patient by Michael Ondaatje*, www.aurochs.org/frbr_example/frbr_example.html.

Miksa, S. (n.d.) *Introduction to Resource Description and Access: cataloguing and classification in the digital era*, Facet Publishing, forthcoming.

NACO (2011) *NACO: the name authority program component of the PCC*, last updated 14 April 2011, www.loc.gov/catdir/pcc/naco/nacopara.html.

OCLC Research (2011) *VIAF (The Virtual International Authority File)*, last updated March 2011, www.oclc.org/research/activities/viaf/.

Oliver, C. (2010) *Introducing RDA: a guide to the basics*, Facet Publishing.

Patton, G.E. (2009) *Functional Requirements for Authority Data: a conceptual model*, IFLA.

Pearson, D. (1998) *Provenance Research in Book History: a handbook*, British Library.

Prytherch, R. (1995) *Harrod's Librarians' Glossary: 9,000 Terms Used in Information Management, Library Science, Publishing, the Book Trades and Archive Management*, 8th edn, Gower.

Program for Cooperative Cataloging Policy Committee (2011) *PoCo Discussion Paper on RDA Implentation Alternatives*, last updated 5 April 2011, www.loc.gov/catdir/pcc/PoCo-RDA-Discussion-Paper040511.pdf.

Ranganathan, S. R. (1989) *Classified Catalogue Code: with additional rules for dictionary catalogue code*, 5th edn, Sarada Ranganathan Endowment for Library Science.

Ranganathan, S. R. (1957) *The Five Laws of Library Science*, 2nd edn, Asia Publishing House.

Sanchez, E. (2010) *[Survey Results]*, www.surveymonkey.com/sr.aspx?sm=lyKPc8gLqpITF_2fK8K127v7qTJG7nV8OD AEclJJOthnQ_3d.

Sanchez, E. (2011) AACR2, RDA and You: your thoughts, *Amigos RDA@Your Library*

Online Conference, 4 February, www.slideshare.net/es02/sanchez-presentationfinalrev5.

Taylor, A.G. (2006) *Introduction to Cataloging and Classification*, 10th edn, Library and Information Science Text Series, Libraries Unlimited.

Taylor, A.G. (ed.) (2007) *Understanding FRBR: what it is and how it will affect our retrieval tools*, Libraries Unlimited.

Terras, M. (2006) *Image to Interpretation: intelligent systems to aid historians in the reading of the Vindolanda Texts*, Oxford Studies in Ancient Documents, Oxford University Press.

Tillett, B. B. (2007) FRBR and RDA: resource description and access. In Taylor, A. G. (ed.), *Understanding FRBR: what it is and how it will affect out retrieval tools*, Libraries Unlimited.

Tillett, B. B. (2008) *A Review of the Feasibility of an International Standard Authority Data Number (ISADN): prepared for the IFLA Working Group on Functional Requirements and Numbering of Authority Records*, IFLA, http://archive.ifla.org/VII/d4/franar-numbering-paper.pdf.

UCL (2006) *Lord Byron Manuscript Discovered*, University College London, www.ucl.ac.uk/news/news-articles/0601/06010502.

US RDA Test Coordinating Committee (2011) *Report and Recommendations of the US RDA Test Coordinating Committee, 9 May 2011*, revised for public release 20 June 2011, www.loc.gov/bibliographic-future/rda/source/rdatesting-finalreport-20june2011. pdf.

Welsh, A. (2009) *FRBR and RDA*, lecture slides, University College London.

Index